MODERN YUGOSLAV
SATIRE

Other Books by Branko Mikasinovich

INTRODUCTION TO YUGOSLAV LITERATURE (1973)

FIVE MODERN YUGOSLAV PLAYS (1977)

MODERN YUGOSLAV SATIRE

edited with an introduction by

BRANKO MIKASINOVICH

Cross-Cultural Communications
Merrick, New York
1979

Published by
Cross-Cultural Communications
239 Wynsum Avenue, Merrick, N.Y. 11566
(516) 868-5635

Publisher: Stanley H. Barkan. *Associate Editor:* Eva Feiler. *Art Editors:* Bebe Barkan, George Zimmermann. *Editorial Board:* David B. Axelrod, Joseph Bruchac, Edward Butscher, Roy Cravzow, Enid Dame, Arthur Dobrin, J. C. Hand, Ko Won, Aaron Kramer, Donald Lev, Ifeanyi A. Menkiti, Raymond R. Patterson, Nat Scammacca, Hans van de Waarsenburg, Joost de Wit.

First Edition
Library of Congress Catalog Card Number: 79-83730
ISBN 0-89304-029-0 Clothbound
ISBN 0-89304-030-4 Paperback

Designed by Bebe Barkan
Printed in the United States of America

To Marijana

Preface

This anthology of contemporary Yugoslav satire introduces the most representative post-war Yugoslav satirists—Serbian, Croatian, Slovenian, and Macedonian. It is the first book of Yugoslav satire to be published in the English language. The order of authors is chronological, and their inclusion is based solely on literary merit.

I wish to express my thanks to Professor Slobodan Sv. Miletić of the University of Novi Sad, Professor Miroslav Egerić of the University of Belgrade, and Professor Vasa D. Mihailovich of the University of North Carolina at Chapel Hill.

A special note of gratitude is due to Mr. Jacob Steinberg, the founder and former president of Twayne Publishers of New York, who was instrumental in the publication of my two previous books, and to Stanley H. Barkan for his careful editing of this manuscript.

Grateful acknowledgment is also accorded as follows for permission to reprint copyright material: "On Yugoslavs," "On Success and Failure," "On Nations," "On Issuing Statements," "On Backwardness" from *Che: A Permanent Tragedy* by Matija Bećković and Dušan Radović, copyright © 1970 by Harcourt Brace Jovanovich, Inc. Reprinted by permission of the publisher; excerpts from *The Strange Story of the Great Whale, Also Known as Big Mac,* copyright © 1972 by Erih Koš, translated by Lovett F. Edwards. Reprinted by permission of Harcourt Brace Jovanovich, Inc.; "The King of Poets" from *New Writings in Yugoslavia,* edited by Bernard Johnson, Penguin Books, 1970. Reprinted by permission of the author.

B. M.

A Note on Pronunciation and Spelling

(Serbo-Croatian, Slovenian, Macedonian)

c =	as in mats
$\check{c}$ =	as in charge
$\acute{c}$ =	similar to, but lighter than, $\check{c}$ —as in arch
$dj,\ d\check{z}$ =	as in George
g =	as in go
j =	as in yell
k =	as in key
lj =	as in million
nj =	as in minion
s =	s as in sink
$\check{s}$ =	as in shift
z =	as in zodiac
$\check{z}$ =	as in measure

Table of Contents

Preface vii

A Note on Pronunciation and Spelling viii

Introduction by Branko Mikasinovich xi

VLADAN DESNICA 1
   Mr. Pink's Soliloquy 2
   Translated by Petar Mijusković

ERIH KOŠ 11
   The Strange Story of the Great Whale, also Known as
     Big Mac (Excerpts) 12
   Translated by Lovett F. Edwards

BRANKO ĆOPIĆ 44
   The Election of Comrade Sokrat 45
   Translated by Branko Mikasinovich

JOŽA HORVAT 49
   Mousehole (Excerpt from *A Cat with a Helmet*) 50
   Translated by Celia Williams

DOBRICA ĆOSIĆ 68
   Freedom 69
   Translated by Muriel Heppel

DUŠAN RADOVIĆ 90
   Monkeys 91
   A Little Finger 92
   Translated by Branko Mikasinovich

VASA POPOVIĆ 94
   The Fenced Sea 95
   Translated by Branko Mikasinovich

ALEKSANDAR POPOVIĆ 99
   Hats Off! 100
   Translated by E.J. Czerwinski

ŽARKO PETAN 147
   Aphorisms 148
   Translated by Vasa D. Mihailovich

VLADA BULATOVIĆ-VIB............................149
   The Illness......................................150
   The Shark and the Bureaucrat........................152
   The Municipal Whale................................154
   Lavatore and Bureaucratsia..........................156
   The Ugly Duckling..................................158
   Translated by Nada Ćurćija-Prodanović

BORA ĆOSIĆ..160
   The King of the Poets...............................161
   Translated by Harold Norminton

BRANA CRNČEVIĆ....................................168
   Write as You Are Silent..............................169
   Translated by Vasa D. Mihailovich

   Prosperity...171
   Translated by Branko Mikasinovich

   Aphorisms..173
   Translated by Vasa D. Mihailovich

ŽIVKO ČINGO..175
   The Medal..176
   Translated by Donald Davenport

SLOBODAN SV. MILETIĆ..............................183
   A Big Et Cetera.....................................184
   Translated by Branko Mikasinovich

MATIJA BEĆKOVIĆ...................................187
   On Yugoslavs.......................................188
   On Success and Failure..............................191
   On Nations...193
   On Issuing Statements...............................195
   On Backwardness...................................198
   Translated by Drenka Willen

TOMAŽ ŠALAMUN....................................200
   Who Is Who...201
   Translated by the author and Anselm Hollo

MILOVAN VITEZOVIĆ................................203
   Aphorisms..204
   Translated by Branko Mikasinovich

Index of Authors, Translators, and Titles..................xvii
About the Editor..xix

Introduction

Everything is clear, and everything is unclear
Common sense has formulated what is clear
What is unclear results from a lack of common sense.

—Matija Bećković

THE LITERATURE OF A COUNTRY enhances its value and importance by the variety of its genres and literary expressions. A literature devoid of satire is seriously lacking. Unlike other literary manners which emphasize what is real, satire emphasizes what seems to be real and is not; its essence is the revelation of the contrast between reality and pretense. Generally, the most common topics of satire are human destiny and politics. The former dwells on such topics as stupidity, sickness, social pressures, old age, uncertainty, a feeling of helplessness, and the loss of one's identity; the latter, on the political arena and all of its implications relating to court, church, authority, and government. This connection between human destiny and politics usually produces the sharpest and most controversial satire. Thus, the quality and the very existence of satire depends on the satirist's ability to seize upon these inconsistencies.

A satirist is a man who expresses his observations and bitterness to everybody—if such an action is justified—for he sees a possibility of improving the world surrounding him. To a satirist, in terms of freedom, mankind is divided into three categories: those who long to be free; those who try to limit freedom; and those who function within the system, be it social or political. By the nature of his work, a satirist belongs to the avant-garde forces of his society. He is a man who is often willing to risk his means of existence and even his life. A satirist is above all else a free man: free in his actions and thoughts. The kind of satirist a man becomes is also determined to a large extent by his environment. Strict censorship forces him to create ingenious ways of circumventing authority. This development of his art may offer new techniques or encourage the use of old ones. All times are out of joint to the satirist. Even in the most congenial period, there is an enormous amount of pretense, hypocrisy, and artificiality in society, and the satirist concentrates on these conditions.

The basic technique of satirical writing is ridicule; it deliberately diminishes the splendor and the glory of the subject depicted. Thus, a king may be made to resemble a beggar, or a legend may be transformed into an illusion. This is why the satirist himself is often the target of ostracism and revenge.

In Yugoslavia, the existence and importance of satire fluctuates with the political climate. Its origin can be traced to the famous letters of the Yugoslav language reformer Vuk Stefanović-Karadjić (1787-1864) to the Serbian Prince, Miloš Obrenović, in which Vuk rebelled against the blindness of Miloš's tyranny. Radoje Domanović (1873-1908) exposed and ridiculed the Serbia of his time, only to pay for it with great personal hardships throughout his life and an early death. Domanović is celebrated for a volume of allegorical stories, *The Land of Stradia* (1902), in which he describes an imaginary country where the loyalty and value of its subjects are estimated according to the amount of oppression they can bear and the number of decorations adorning the breasts of their oppressors. The masses in Stradia blindly follow the leaders, unable to see that the leaders too are blind. Branislav Nušić (1864-1938) is best known for his humorous and satirical pieces on the political life in Serbia, such as *The Suspicious Character* (1887), *Favoritism* (1889), *An Ordinary Man* (1900), and *The Municipal Child* (1902). Bosnian Petar Kočić (1887-1916), who wrote relatively little, became famous for his satire "The Badger on Trial" (1904) in which the legal system and formalism of Austro-Hungary are ridiculed. It is a history of an inconspicuous, rather stupid-looking Bosnian peasant who sues a badger for damages. With this vehicle of the trial of the badger, Kočić praised the common sense of the peasant and condemned Austrian justice.

As a whole, Yugoslav satire had not been encouraged during the 19th century nor was it at the beginning of the 20th century. While

Serbian satire was often stifled by domestic regimes, Croatian and Slovenian satire were stifled by foreign domination. The early satirical achievements in Croatia are associated with the names of Ante Kovačić (1854-1889) and Miroslav Krleža (b. 1893), and, in Slovenia, with Fran Levstik (1831-1887). Kovačić, both in literature and politics, followed Ante Starčević, a noted radical Croatian politician and *littérateur* with an inflexible style. In his satirical works, Kovačić depicted the falseness and hypocrisy of the town philanthropists, who were in fact tyrants and exploiters of the poor. He exposed the misery of government employees and the vanity of the superficial intelligentsia. In Krleža's literary output, a special place is occupied by *The Songs of Perica Kerempuh* (1936). In a series of poems written in a Croatian dialect—*Kajkavski*—Krleza produces a synthetic picture of the whole tragic past of the Croat, whom the feudal lords, the church, and the bourgeoisie had tormented for centuries and who was even deceived by his cultural leaders. One of the founders of Slovene prose, Fran Levstik exhibited luminous imagery and a sense of humor. His *Martin Kerpan of Verkh* (1858) is a novella based on a folk tale about a Slovene peasant of enormous physical strength, who, single-handedly saves the emperor from his enemy in Vienna. At the end, Martin's reward is being allowed to carry salt openly from one place to another, an article which he had always previously smuggled.

After the Second World War, when the war and revolution changed the Yugoslav social structure, satire acquired a new and different dimension. With the idea of a classless society and the imminent goal of reconstructing Yugoslavia following the war's devastation, neither political nor other circumstances fostered the development of satire. From 1945 to 1948, when Yugoslavia broke from the Soviet Union, Yugoslav literature was founded on "Socialist Realism," the most frequent topics of which were war, reconstruction, and social change. As a whole, however, Yugoslavs rejected the Soviet notion that the single criterion to judge a literature is its social usefulness. In the early 50's, Yugoslavs affirmed the principle of freedom of creation, especially in form and expression. A trend of liberation emerged, and some satirical writings started to appear. However, satire—even then—was most often regarded from the old orthodox perspective and treated as a negative literary genre. Because it did not show the action of some essential force—as did comedy, tragedy, and epic—but instead portrayed the absence of good sense and the loss of traditional values, Yugoslav satire of this period was a blend of amusement and unpleasant facts. Unlike Russian satire, which was generally described as "optimistic," Yugoslav satire was mostly "critical."

Post-war Yugoslav satire could not have existed without the various satirical and humorous journals, which usually mounted campaigns against various social problems—the hooligan, bribery, and embezzlement of money. Throughout the post-war period, the satirical spirit sustained itself on a much larger scale, frequently orally, especially as a political joke or an anecdote. This oral satire served as a complement to written satire. Eventually, oral satire found its way into the Belgrade satirical magazine *Jež* (The Hedgehog), which became one of the main outlets of Yugoslav post-war satire.

Branko Ćopić (b. 1915), who started writing satire in the early 50's, should be credited with initiating post-war Yugoslav satire. Like most of his other writings, Ćopić's satire is simple and pointed. It contains a message similar to an oral tale. The tale is supposed to have a moral, but the point gets lost on the way; so it is himself he expresses and not the moral. It is a technique derived from popular story-telling. The narrator, whom we come to understand through the words and expressions he uses and misuses— his repetitions, digressions, the things he chooses to talk about, and the things that read between the lines—injects himself very much into the story. The writers cultivating this type of satire are Branko Ćopić, Vasa Popović, and to a degree, Matija Bećković.

The second and by far the most popular type of Yugoslav satire is intellectual satire, often referred to as "cynical." This is a form of satire dominated by bitterness about the disproportion between reality and idealism. The subjects of such satirical pieces are the most common occurrences of everyday Yugoslav life. They are situations familiar to all Yugoslavs: housing shortage, bureaucracy, the juxtaposition of backwardness and material progress, and other social and cultural events.

These traditional themes are not merely the background of the stories, but also the determining force; they shape or obliterate motives, they expose and frustrate, and they are inevitable. They demonstrate that nature and other superior forces are still with us, regardless of the type of society we live in. This type of satirical writing is characterized by its irony and seriousness. However, this satire is not the dry, impersonal condemnation it seems, but is instead humorous and human. This "humorous-but-human" satire played a very important political role: it was one of the major forces in the de-Stalinization of post-war Yugoslav literature. Not only was it on the side of freedom, but it also did its share in acquiring that freedom. This is the satire of Erih Koš, Mateja Bećković, Brana Crnčević, Vlada Bulatović-Vib, Ježa Horvat, Vladan Desnica, Dobrica and Bora Ćosić, Vasa Popović, Žarko Petan, Tomaž Šalamun, and Milovan Vitezović.

Another aspect of Yugoslav satire is represented here by the writings of Aleksandar Popović. Popović, the creator of some of the most unusual characters of Serbian satirical and dramatic literature, is considered to be the founder of Yugoslav dramatic satire. He is the undisputed master in creating the grotesque and vulgar, as is evidenced in his play *Hats Off!*, a protest against mechanization, bureaucracy, and automated life and sex.

As if to mirror the fast pace of industrialized consumer society, Yugoslav satirists expressed themselves primarily through short pieces: short stories, poems, and aphorisms. These forms allow a rapid exchange of expressions and experiences. Erih Koš's and Alekasandar Popović's long satirical works are striking exceptions. The short satirical forms of, for instance, Bećković, Bulatović, Crnčević, Šalamun, Petan, and Desnica reiterate one of the fundamentals of Yugoslav satire, especially of the later post-war period: that art on the one hand, and moral judgment on the other are never two separate entities. Together they form a vital and appealing whole.

—BRANKO MIKASINOVICH

New Orleans
January, 1979

VLADAN DESNICA

(1905-1963)

Desnica was born in Zadar and received his law degree from the University of Zagreb. Up to the Second World War, he wrote extensively but published little. He translated lyrics, prose, and philosophical works from Italian and French. After the Second World War, he published a number of short-story collections: *Derelicts in the Sun* (1952), *Here Just Behind Us* (1956), and *The Springtime of Ivan Galeb* (1960).

"Mr. Pink's Soliloquy" shows Desnica's predilection for irony and self-analytic intellectualism. This story is one of the best examples of Desnica's satire, from both the literary and intellectual standpoints.

His writings are complex but carefully structured; they are written with a scientist's clarity and precision—plots, themes, and images are skillfully manipulated and dynamically developed. His language is rich and flexible, ranging from classical simplicity to an ultra-sophisticated style.

Mr. Pink's Soliloquy

WHILE I WORK, I usually listen to my radio. Some people can't stand it while they're working. My colleague, Bermut, for instance, says he'd never be able to get any work done that way. On the contrary, it doesn't bother me a bit. I suppose I'm used to it. If the music interests me, I work and listen at the same time; if it doesn't, I stop hearing it by automatically switching off my attention.

When I'm at home in the afternoon, I work till nightfall. It's rather tiring, so it's no wonder if I'm absent-minded in a way. They say one type of work is a rest from another. I'm a clerk at the Export Bank. I work the whole morning, and at home I work for Continental the whole afternoon. Always the same old accountancy grind. They trust me, so they let me take my books home, especially if there's a two-day holiday. This usually happens when a feast day or national holiday comes after a Sunday. Bands play in the streets, troops march by, but I sit at home engrossed in Continental's accounts, by way of resting up for the Export Bank. For a bachelor, this is supposed to be recreation, but at times it fags me out completely.

Last Sunday, for instance, I worked at home the whole morning and afternoon for Continental. I wanted to get the work done at all costs. I went out to lunch at one, and, when I got back, I was astonished to hear my radio going full strength; so I hurried in to turn it down. You know how the neighbors yell their heads off and thump on the ceiling with their brooms for quiet when someone pounds the piano or plays the radio loudly at midday. I went on with my work till evening, when I went out again to have dinner and take a walk in the fresh air. Now, I remember distinctly taking special care to turn off the radio before I left. Being absent-minded, I delay a lot on my way out, fiddle about in the corridor in front of the door of my flat, and go over in my mind the things I might have forgotten to do. I see to the gas two or three times, the water tap, the electric light (especially the light in the lavatory which is so easy to leave burning). There are times when I even return up the stairs to have a last look around. There's nothing easier than forgetting the electric cooker, especially if it is the kind with a covered-in top and you can't see the wires. A friend of mine once went off on a five-day trip for Easter with his wife, but, when they were on the train, they simply couldn't get it out of their heads that they had forgotten to turn off a small electric heater. Unable to stand it any longer, they hurried back after three days. Of course they hadn't forgotten the heater at all.

Well, anyway, before going out on Sunday evening I was careful to switch off my radio. And I'm quite sure I had switched it off. I might have left the gas on, I might have forgotten the cooker after making myself a cup of tea. I might even have left the door un-locked. (That's another reason why I often go upstairs again— sometimes even twice.) But I'm doubly sure I had switched off the radio. You will understand me when I say I was particularly careful to do so because I had forgotten it at noon. To make certain, I remember trying to memorize the last words I heard before turning it off: *This disease used to play havoc with orchards. We now have many means with which to combat it, the most efficacious be-ing*... and, at this point, I had turned the knob, cutting the an-nouncer's speech in half. As I was going down the stairs, I repeated the words and asked myself what those "most efficacious" means might be. I should have listened at least till I had heard what they were. And then something kept nagging at me for not having done so.

So you can imagine my surprise when, having got back home that evening, I found my radio on! I was going up the stairs when I heard the soft strings of a tango. Surely it isn't mine, I said to myself. I went in, trembling with apprehension. And indeed it was mine: from the small entry foyer, I saw its glowing indicator. It was playing a tango quite softly—but it was playing, all right.

I must say I felt uneasy. I searched the flat, looked into every corner, and even under the bed. What occurred to me was that someone had broken into my flat during my absence. The charwoman, who cleans for me twice a week, has the unfortunate habit of forgetting to lock the small balcony on which she keeps her brooms, mops, and other odds and ends, and a thief might easily slip in by that way—it's a perfect way for him to enter. But the door to the balcony was locked. Another idea: the thief might have found the door unlocked, entered the flat, and locked the door behind him. But there was no one in the flat: I searched again—nowhere a sign of anyone. If he had left by the same way, the door would have been unlocked. But the radio was playing! Softly, to be sure, but it was playing all right. Then I thought that maybe there was something wrong with the control knob. I didn't feel much conviction in that idea. But I tried to reason it out: maybe the control knob was loose, maybe it switched off easily, and then, when the current increased after housewives have finished cooking dinner (is that what they call "tension"?—I must admit that physics is not my strong point), it attracts the control knob over the "on" side. Anyway, I decided I'd call at the electrician's at the corner on my way to the office the next morning. I know him, and I always ask him to repair my cooker when the wire burns out. He's a nice man, a stout, good-natured fellow, and he always says "Good morning" to me as I pass. I switched off the radio and went to bed.

The next morning I dropped in at the electrician's. "Impossible!" he broke in on my explanation. Probably his other customers have often asked the same question. I don't know why, but the thought that I wasn't the only one was comforting.

There was no other explanation. I must have forgotten to turn off the control knob, that's all. Sometimes a man intends to do something and the intention slips out of his mind, and he's sure he has done what he intended to do. That is the only logical explanation. Maybe there are some other logical explanations, too.

Being a bachelor and not given much to company, I often spend my time trying to get to the bottom of different problems, including problems that don't concern me, and working out different answers to them. And then, sometimes, I reflect over the things that haven't really happened but only might have. I see something in the street or hear something at the office, anything at all, about someone else's business, about an accident, a strange event, or something like that, and then I begin to think about it and go on thinking about it, imagining how it might develop. I imagine, for instance, a tiny detail being omitted, or a different course followed; and then I unwind the thread, deduce the consequences, and you simply can't believe what strange things occur, what unbelievable results are arrived at, what unexpected endings come out. Sometimes you only need to change an accidental and apparently negligible circumstance to bring about a terrible tragedy.

Chance can really contrive all sorts of strange things, so strange that human fancy is incapable of conceiving them. The following story is an instance:

Three children were playing at home. Their mother had gone shopping, their father was looking for a job. Well, children being what they are, they climbed into an old-fashioned trunk with the intention, I suppose, of surprising their mother when she got back. They heard steps on the stairs and thought they were their mother's. They expected her to come, stop in surprise at not finding them, look in all the rooms, hesitate wordless in the middle of the kitchen, and finally ask herself where they could have hidden. They then would jump out of their hiding place like Indians and shout "Boo!" But, by some accident, it was not their mother climbing the stairs, but a lady from the third floor. By a further accident, the trunk was locked by one of those flaps with a slit in the middle that drops over a loop and is secured with a padlock when the lid is let down. Anyway, the children were as safely locked in the trunk as a mouse in a mousetrap. They screamed, frantic with fright. They pushed and pushed against the lid, but, of course, in vain. If, by chance, the lady next door had come in to borrow some salt (she was always borrowing something, and Mother was always saying things after she left), nothing would have happened; she would have come in (because the flat was not locked and it could be opened by turning the outside knob), she would have heard the children screaming, and she would simply have unfastened the lid. The children would have climbed out wide-eyed with fright; perhaps they would have begged her not to say anything to Mother, and she would have been careful of the trunk and avoided it like the plague. But it happened that the lady next door didn't need any salt. . . . In short, anyone can picture the poor mother on finding her three children smothered in a trunk. It isn't hard to see her looking all over the house for them, imagining all sorts of things, including the impossible, but not the truth; searching everywhere, including the most absurd places, and altogether forgetting the one place she should look. In fact, it is hard to imagine her looking for them in the trunk at all and that anything but chance should direct her footsteps toward it. Probably she would not look there till the following day or even the day after.

Many things might have happened. The neighbors might have heard the children screaming to come to their rescue. Or their mother might have come back from shopping in time. Or, by chance, the flap might not have fallen over the loop, just as by chance it had. All these things might have happened; it was just an accident that they hadn't. Almost everything that happened to us and around us depends entirely on small and insignificant details that might be imagined as happening differently. Possibilities simply teem all around us. We live a life of extreme peril. Everything—absolutely everything—depends on some trivial circumstance, on some negligible turn of our mind, on the minute electrical impulses in our brain cells. Everything hangs on a single thread! Our destiny, our very life, lies in the hand of blind chance. Just imagine that the life of three children, that the happiness and very survival of a whole family may depend on whether the mother remains shopping a few seconds longer (because, for instance, the potatoes at the stall at which she bought her tomatoes are not of the best quality and she must go to another stall for better ones), or the children decide upon their prank at nine twenty-three or at nine twenty-eight, or they play it the day the lady next door needs salt or the day she doesn't, or even on whether the flap on Great-grandmother's old-fashioned trunk is a little more rusty or a little less, and on whether it will drop over the loop at the smallest shock or not. Just as it was the working of blind chance that a slat was missing from the half-rotten back of the trunk, through which sufficient air entered for the wretched children to breathe and survive till their mother returned from shopping. Anyway, that is another circumstance that equally might not have occurred—it was sheer chance that it had.

They say there is no such thing as accident, and I once heard a lengthy explanation to that effect. I remember, I was thoroughly convinced at the time. But now, to tell the truth, I no longer remember how it ran, but I do remember it was quite reasonable and that afterward I had laughed and laughed, assured that there is no such thing as accident. And, indeed, there is no such thing as accident. But there is such a thing as our imagining a given circumstance in two, five, or even a thousand different ways. And it is enough for one single, entirely negligible trifle out of this endless number to be this or that, and the consequence will be nothing at all or a tragedy. Whether the result will be according to one formula or another, we cannot say. This is quite clear to me, and I think most people will agree on this point; but whether this implies that there is such a thing as accident or that there is no such thing, I cannot say.

Forgetfulness and absent-mindedness are also frequently the cause of "accident." As soon as a man is cautious, or the more cunning he becomes in his struggle with forgetfulness or absent-mindedness, the more cunning, the more deceitful, the keener, and the more artful become his forgetfulness or absent-mindedness. Their nets become all the easier to fall into, so that in the long run they win. Doctors say that it is often like this with illness: the more germs you kill, the more resistant the remaining ones become, and the time finally comes when penicillin or whatever it may be no longer works.

And then, what we often term forgetfulness or absent-mindedness is sometimes neither forgetfulness nor absent-mindedness in the true sense of the word, but merely something similar. Something that, when the matter is reconsidered, should rather be called thoughtlessness, criminal carelessness. But, as a rule, we are all, without exception, guilty of carelessness every day. Carelessness, in fact, is quite a normal thing. Indeed, unless it has turned into tragedy it is not really carelessness, and no one thinks of it as such. We calculate that we will get to the other side of the street before a car gets to us. If we calculate correctly, well and good. If not, we are guilty of carelessness, criminal carelessness, unpardonable carelessness, carelessness that even a car will not pardon us for.

I know of one such case. A young mother was bathing her baby in a large basin on the table. She noticed that the water was getting cold. "Baby will catch cold," she thought, and took the basin with the child in it and set it on the gas range, which was turned low. Perhaps she even felt a thrill of pride at her clever idea. Then someone rang the next-door neighbor's doorbell. She knew that the visitor was ringing in vain, as her neighbor had gone to the country to be by the side of her daughter, who was having a baby, and would be away a few days. The unknown visitor was persistent, like a man in an official cap with a sheaf of summonses and receipts in his hand and an indelible pencil stuck behind his ear, like the telegraph boy with a wire, an inspector who threatens to cut off the electricity, an official with a military summons. The unknown visitor kept ringing and ringing, as stubbornly as authority. The young mother hastened to the door for just a second, just long enough to tell him he was ringing in vain, that her neighbor was away from home, and no more. She ran to the door with her wet hands and opened it by pressing on the handle with her elbow.... When would the lady return? She didn't know, probably in a day or two, she'd gone to be with her daughter, who was having a baby. ...And then—Bang! A draft slammed the door shut.

A thing like that can happen. In fact, a thing like that often does happen; a thing we read of in comic books or see at the movies, a thing almost torn to shreds. I remember having read somewhere about someone who was just having a bath when a visitor rang his doorbell. And, when the visitor finally gave up and was already halfway down the stairs, curiosity teased our bather and attracted him, all covered with soap suds, to take a look down the stairwell—and a little breeze slammed the door. I might even say there is no one who hasn't had a similar experience. But sometimes it isn't funny. For instance, if that young mother had had a cherry pie in the oven, she would tell the story often and always give her guests a good laugh. In the matter of carelessness, as I have already said, the point is whether or not there will be any after effects. (But it isn't only a matter of carelessness; there is even something of the appeal of adventure. I tried to convince my colleagues at the bank. "Don't be a fool! No mother is going to risk her child's life because of the adventure!" "Now, don't be so obstinate; I know about these things better than you do," I'd retort heatedly.) So, if the man in the official cap hadn't chanced to be having a baby, there would have been nothing to accuse the young mother of. Or, even if everything had happened as it did, but the wind—a quite imprudent, irresponsible fellow—hadn't slammed the door, no one, of course, would have had anything to say. Someone would have objected, though, if she had not gone to see who was ringing so persistently and to tell him no one was at home.

Fortunately, however, the young mother chanced to have the key to her flat in her apron pocket and unlocked the door, so nothing happened. Anyway, that evening, still half-terrified, half-exhilarated, she told her friend about her adventure, and she, in turn, told it to her husband, and he told it to me at the office the next day.

Well, that's how it is with carelessness. But forgetfulness and absent-mindedness are something different. I only know that every evening now, as I return home, I listen on the stairs for music coming from my flat. I listen with misgiving, as though it were my own voice, the voice of that other self of mine talking to itself inside, the voice of the detached, subconscious half of myself. And, if by chance I do not hear it, I do not attribute this circumstance to myself, but to accident. It's clear enough: ghosts do not exist. The door of the balcony with the broom is duly locked. As for the control knob, however loose it may be, there is no tension strong enough to turn the radio on. That's what the stout electrician at the corner said. Impossible! Therefore, I alone must be the cause of its being turned on. The whole question is: did I forget to turn the knob off or, at a higher level of absent-mindedness, did I forget this? And did I, confused as I am, think I had turned it off while, in fact, I hadn't, but only thought I had, or had I in fact done so, without having given a thought to doing so. And it might be that I really had turned it off and then unconsciously turned it on again. Because a man can force himself to remember what he has consciously and willingly done, but how can he remember what he has done unconsciously? And it is only toward evening, while going upstairs, that I get an answer to the question: I listen keenly for sounds coming from my flat; if the radio is playing, it means I didn't turn it off; if it is not playing, it means I did. And you can't imagine how this trivial unknown quantity that awaits me at the end of the day provokes me. In my lonely life it comes as a kind of entertainment—the only indefinite, uncertain thing in my monotonous life. The only unknown quantity, the only riddle in my life, the only thing that can constitute an uncertainty and a riddle is—myself. Often, as I leave the house, I turn back from the landing torn by doubt: have I locked the door? And usually I find that in my absent-mindedness I have really locked it, quite mechanically. But I don't go back into my flat to see about the radio: if I did, I should be depriving myself of a small, provoking uncertainty, of a pleasant little surprise awaiting me at the end of the day, like a lump of sugar by my bed. But to find that I have indeed locked the door gives me pleasure, I must admit. It pleases me, as though I have cheated someone, and it flatters me, because it bears out my contention that if our absent-mindedness chances to turn out to our advantage, it is a virtue, we are normal, and everything is all right. But, if it doesn't, we're like that wretched mother.

Occasionally, though, I ask myself, is it absent-mindedness or something else? I don't know, I can't say. At any rate, to look at it from a practical point of view, unless something disastrous happens, people will be inclined to believe it is absent-mindedness. Of course! Ordinary absent-mindedness! Why worry your head about it? Things like that happen to me, too, to everyone!

Still, I decided to see a doctor. (How strange, even in one's thoughts one is reluctant to call him by the name of his speciality: I say "a doctor" as though it were a case of bronchitis or heartburn.) But I didn't. And, anyway, what could I say to him? "Doctor, sometimes I forget to turn off my radio." He'd stare at me and say, "Well, what about it?" And he'd look me up and down in a funny sort of way. He'd be suspicious, not because I forget to turn my radio off, but because I came to see him about it. And he'd probably say to himself, "He's not quite right in the head."

No, no! It's better like this. So long as it's like this, I'm "quite right in the head."

Translated by Peter Mijušković

ERIH KOŠ

(b. 1913)

Koš was born in Sarajevo. He graduated from law school in Belgrade where he began his literary career as a reviewer and critic. He participated in the Second World War on the side of the Partisans.

After the war, Koš started writing short stories and novels which concentrated on war topics: *The Time of War* (1952), *Snow and Ice* (1961), and *First Person Singular* (1962).

The turning point in Koš's literary activity was the publication of his social satire, *The Strange Story of the Great Whale, Also Known as Big Mac* (1956), which was acclaimed as a well-paced satire, neatly plotted and sagely characterized. This satire opens simply enough—a whale is found on the Adriatic Coast and is sent on a tour of major Yugoslav cities, with Belgrade being the final destination. Everyone in the city is anxious to view this unusual creature, except an unimportant civil servant. Because of his unwillingness to mingle with others, the hero antagonizes his landlady, mistress, and fellow workers, creating an explosive situation at home and in his office.

In the end, public opinion turns against the whale's vile-smelling carcass, which must be rapidly removed from the city. There is no forgiveness, however, for the hero even though he was right; rather, one can only foresee more trouble because he is different.

The Strange Story
of the Great Whale,
Also Known as Big Mac
(Excerpts)

"IN A DAY OR TWO, *the people of Belgrade will have the chance of visiting an unusual exhibition. A huge whale will be on show, probably in the Zoological Gardens. . . . The whale was captured by the people of Pag late last month.*

"This exhibition will be the most interesting in that whales are not found in the Adriatic. The people of the island only know from the tales of old men that another such sea monster appeared there sixty years ago. It was captured and killed. Today it is in the Vienna Museum.

"The dead whale had already been on show at Rijeka, and then at Ljubljana and Zagreb. About 150,000 people saw it."

—POLITIKA, February 10, 1953

***

"The whale was on show yesterday in Proletarian Brigade Street. . . . How huge this Leviathan is may be judged from the size of its head. It is roughly eighty feet long. The mouth is so big that a child of about seven or eight could sit in it quite comfortably, and there is room in it for four or five men if they lie beside one another."

—POLITIKA, February 15, 1953

***

12

"The whale will be on show in our capital for five or six days. Tickets will cost: Individuals, 25 dinars; for group visits, 10 dinars each. School children, soldiers, and students, 15 dinars."

—POLITIKA, February 15, 1953

***

"The whale on exhibition . . . has aroused great interest among the people of Belgrade. Though the weather was bad yesterday, with soft snowfalls, up to five in the afternoon, about twenty thousand people went to see the monster. There was so great a crowd that vehicles could not pass along the street. Even after dusk had fallen, there were long queues of people at the ticket offices waiting to get in. The whale can be seen at night because it has been floodlit."

—POLITIKA, February 16, 1953

***

"The whale is the largest of the sea mammals. It breathes with lungs like land mammals. It lives in the oceans, but only up to the limits of the ice pack, since every three-and-a-half minutes it must come to the surface to breathe in air, and then it dives again. It grows to about ninety feet in length and to a weight of about one-hundred-and-forty-five tons. It has its young in the usual manner, and the female gives birth to a calf twenty to twenty-five feet long, which it suckles. So that the calf may suck, the female has a sort of pouch at the base of which are the milk glands and into which the young whale inserts itself. The calf takes hold of the teat and the mother by muscular action pumps the milk into its mouth.

How do whales get into the Adriatic? They come to us as visitors from the Atlantic Ocean."

—POLITIKA, February 18, 1953

When I came home from the office that day, my landlady opened the door, and, while I was hanging up my coat (the loop had broken and needed mending), she asked me:

"Mr. Rade! Did you read the papers today! Did you see that the fishermen have caught a whale?"

She led a dull life. Of her three lodgers, I was the only one who came home in the afternoon, and she usually waylaid me in the passage or hall, eager for a long conversation, whereas I, tired out from my work at the office, from bookkeeping and talking to callers and hungry after the rotten meal in the canteen, was in a hurry to lie down and get a few moments' sleep as soon as I could. I felt overcome by hunger and fatigue and the need to digest the heavy food—canteen beans and smoked meat. So this time, too, fumbling about in the half-light for the coat rack, while she stood waiting to one side and taking advantage of my trouble with my overcoat which I could not manage to hang up, I replied curtly and ill-humoredly:

"Rubbish! A whale indeed! Why, there aren't any in our seas. It's some nonsense thought up by the newspapers. I never heard of such a thing."

"Nonsense, indeed! So it's all idle gossip, is it?" she interrupted. "You might at least read the papers first. They even have pictures; you don't mean to tell me that the pictures are lies. Anyhow, who said it came from our seas? Perhaps it came from foreign parts."

Then she began to chatter to me about all sorts of whales. She spoke passionately, with knowledge and conviction; of white and blue whales, of sperm whales, killer whales, of whales that live on plankton and others which swallow big fish, of whales that live only in cold seas and others, rarer ones, sometimes found in warm waters. It was evident that she had read the newspapers thoroughly and that the journalist had looked up his facts in some reference book.

It seemed to me boorish and ill-mannered that she should take advantage of my confusion, letting me struggle with the hall stand in the semidarkness, and mocking me as if enjoying my predicament, while she went on chattering and gossiping without a pause instead of turning on the light, for the switch was well within her reach. I had to turn around to pick up my coat, which had fallen on the floor, and, angered by this, I said to her roughly, more roughly than I should, that this whale meant nothing to me. Devil take both it and the newspaper (and her, too, I thought to myself). Did she think I had nothing better to do than to worry about such things, that I had nothing better to do than think about whales! I must have said all this pretty forcefully, for she said nothing and, when I had finally succeeded in hanging up my coat and rushed into my room so that I should not see it if it fell down again, she remained silent for a moment and moved aside to let me pass. But that didn't stop her from shouting after me:

"How pigheaded you are! You can deny now that whales come here, too!"

I had become excited, foolishly and without reason. I knew that I would only get to sleep with difficulty. My nerves must be out of order if I get upset by such trifles. They make me bad-tempered. I get angry and tremble all over for no reason at all; my whole body quivers and every nerve is on edge. It takes me a long time to cool down. I keep on trying to avoid or prevent it. In spite of myself, I fall into this sort of irritable mood at the slightest, quite unimportant thing. Especially if someone tries to give me detailed explanations, goes on trying to prove something, and makes every effort to assure and convince me. I feel as if everyone were trying to gang up on me, to conspire against me. They are always thinking up something and then changing their minds, and then, when I haven't even been able to understand what they first said, they tell me that it is out of date, that I must look for something new, perfect, modern, without giving me time to consider and weigh everything slowly, at my ease, and without letting me rely on my own feelings and common sense. I feel confused and topsy-turvy, like a fly, and I seem like some semiliterate lout at the movies who cannot follow the captions on the screens and hasn't managed to read the first line before the second takes its place. I feel like putting my fingers in my ears, running away, or standing and shouting: "Leave me in peace—let me think it over!"

The main thing was that I knew I no longer had any hope of sleeping. And when I stretched myself out on the divan, I felt myself shivering. It must be because I'm tired, I thought to myself, from a hard day at the office, from the endless answers and explanations, from the exhaustion that I have been feeling for some time past. I know I ought to go to a doctor, to see if he can help me.

Then I tried to convince myself that it was because of lack of food, for the lunch in the canteen was nothing to write home about. But that didn't help; it was the end of the month and my pockets were empty, so that I couldn't even hope for a good supper. I resolutely chased away such unconsoling thoughts and tried to daydream about the sea. I would bathe under the palms in the warm southern sea. This had always helped when I had to calm myself and get to sleep. So I tried to lull myself into sleep.

I lay on the divan in the chill, cheerless room, covered by a thin blanket, with a cushion under my head and my hand over my eyes to shield them from the bright light. I had taken off my coat and put on my pajama top, but had kept on my trousers, though I knew I ought to press them, and felt that to be a weakness of will and a singular proof of a laziness that weighed upon my conscience. But sleep would not come; I kept remembering first my trousers, which were getting creased, and then the callers at the office; my landlady, with her old-maidish toothless smile and the combs in her untidy hair, kept swimming back into my consciousness; and when I finally managed to dive into that warm sea and swam in it, rocking myself pleasantly and easily, feeling that the warm stream was lulling me to sleep, a black mass appeared before my eyes, a mountain of flesh, a whale which spouted a twin fountain from its nostrils, and around it sailing-boats just as I had seen them in some children's book. It seemed to me that I was in one of those skiffs, rowing with all my strength and shouting out, "Strike him! Strike him!" when the whale suddenly leaped out of the water and flapped its tail and capsized me into the chill sea. I struggled to come to the surface, but, as soon as I opened my eyes, I knew that it was all up with my sleep. My blanket had fallen off, my feet were frozen, and I felt that I had caught a cold.

By this time it was already four o'clock, and I had to be back at the office by five. The room seemed even colder and more cheerless in the early twilight; there was nothing to keep me there, and I decided to go out and stroll about the streets, to look at the shop windows and the girls.

So I got up and made my way to the bathroom to wash and brush up. It was quiet in the flat. The landlady must have gone to lie down, to enjoy the sleep, which she had deprived me of, and I banged the doors intentionally to waken her. On my way through the hall, I saw the morning paper on the table, among the landlady's scissors, tape measures, scraps and patterns, and other sewing paraphernalia; I couldn't stop myself from picking it up and taking it into my room. I sat down by the window and began to glance at it, skimming through it before going out. Nothing special. Elections and riots in countries far enough away from ours, diplomatic affairs incomprehensible to the average man, articles about some factory or other, legal advice, market news, preparation for the spring sowing, and then, in the center of the page, a headline:

GREAT WHALE AT SEA NEAR SPLIT

across three columns, and underneath:

"SPLIT, March 20. The fishermen, who have now been able to set to sea because of the better weather, have told us that they have twice seen the big whale. It dived and then surfaced, spouting sprays of water. Men in the nearest boat considered that it was an exceptionally large whale, like those usually seen only in the waters around the North Pole. Since the boats had no equipment for hunting so great a deep-sea monster, a few rifle shots were fired at the whale, but without any evident results.

Beneath the text was a rather misty picture of an indistinct black form from which nothing could be gathered. Under the picture was "The whale at sea." The article continued:

"It is believed that this unusual visit has been caused by the hard weather, which has brought the whale into our waters, where it has been wandering among the islands and is now trying to find its way back to the open sea. It is thought that the whale has frightened the fish, which may be the reason for the recent poor catches. The fishermen have, therefore, decided to organize a hunt for the whale, in the hope that, if they succeed in catching it, it will make up for the losses they have sustained."

So they hadn't caught it yet! Since I had begun by snapping at my landlady, I was pleased that there was nothing to be seen in the picture and that the whale had not yet been caught. I got up and washed, feeling almost aggrieved that I did not meet her in the hall so that I could tell her. I left the newspaper on the table, picked up my hat, and went into the street.

It was a nice evening, and I at once felt better tempered. Such trivialities—which incidentally showed I had been right—are enough to put a man in a good temper. I smiled to myself, found it easy and pleasant working with my colleague, and we quickly finished all we had to do. I was waiting for him, too, to ask questions about the whale. I felt that he was just going to, but then, for some reason or other, perhaps because the whole thing seemed silly and unimportant, he refrained. I felt tempted to complain to him about the people around us, who were always greedy for sensations, and to blame the papers for having nothing better to do than dream up stories about whales. I wanted to pat myself on the back because I had always doubted the landlady's stories, but I didn't want my colleague to think I was really interested in whales. As so many other times when I had decided to do nothing, I found I had already done it; I told him all that I had heard about the whale and, I am ashamed to say, added a few details of what I knew about whales. "They think up all this nonsense," I said, "just to attract readers. They chatter about whales, and the people, just because it is something new and strange, big and unusual, are always ready to be interested, instead of concerning themselves with things right under their noses and in reach of their hands. Our streets are covered with snow and warmer days will be here soon, but one never dreams of rolling up his sleeves and sweeping the pavements...." I went on speaking for some time, longer than I had intended, but my colleague did not smile at my sallies nor agree with my comments. He only looked at me with green eyes and red-rimmed, probably inflamed, lids, and nodded.

"Interesting," he said. "I am sorry that I never noticed this whale, though I read the papers carefully; I must look out for it and read about it when I get home."

That was all he said. I got the impression that he was even hurrying home to pick up the paper as soon as possible. He would not stop at the café for a drink, nor go for a walk so that we could continue our conversation. So I went home myself, in a worse temper than before, and firmly decided that I would not say anything more

about the whale, even if I were asked. And with that resolution I
went to sleep in the chilly room.

I woke as though I had just had a nightmare. I succeeded in getting out of the flat without meeting the landlady. I had a heavy day;
I was balancing the accounts and spent all my time with my nose
glued to my books. (But when I had passed the newspaper kiosk, I
couldn't help buying a paper; I had opened it in the street, looked
through it carefully, and concluded with satisfaction that there was
nothing in it about the whale.) Till noon I didn't speak a word to
anyone, and then, as bad luck would have it, in came the typist,
Tsana, who had recently been hanging around me in so open a
manner that even the others had noticed. She seized a moment
when I raised my head to smile at me, and then sat down opposite.
"I was thinking a lot about you yesterday," she said, "almost all
day." Really, I wondered to myself, and what have I to thank for
that? "You see, I was reading the papers and remembered that you
came from the coast. Did you read that bit about the whale?"

I was offended. What had I to do with the whale and why should
only it remind her of me? But it was not just that which made me
shake my head; it was partly because of my decision not to talk
about the whale any more, partly because of my contrary and ill-
humored nature, which always drives me to belittle anything others
praise, that something in me that prevents me from joining in when
others shout, "Long live someone or other" or "Bravo!," a spite-
ful, secret, destructive urge that makes me jeer when I should be
sad and, against my will, twist my mouth into a smile at any
moving or important moment when I ought to be serious and sad
like everybody else—all these things conspired to catch me off
balance, and made me, foolishly and unnecessarily, shake my head.

"No, I didn't read it. In what paper?"

I felt I had made a mistake, but it was too late; I could not draw
back. My colleague, the bookkeeper with whom I had been working last night, was sitting at the next desk. He must have heard
everything and could give me away. Tsana went on loudly:

"You must have read it! It was in POLITIKA! Illustrated, with a
picture. A real great foreign whale on a visit to our seas."

I felt compelled to express my wonder and astonishment, to lie
and to pretend that I knew nothing about it, while all the time com-

paring what she was saying with what I had read in the papers. The story grew on her lips. She embroidered it shamelessly; the whale grew suddenly from yesterday to today and was already a "gigantic monster." It had come from foreign seas and had almost capsized the fishing boats that had set out to catch it. "Those fine lads might have gotten hurt!" she said, looking at me, looking me up and down in a way that made me feel uncomfortable, and then facing me while opening and closing her fat, fleshy knees, which showed under her raised skirt, like a lobster when it catches something in its claws.

"I thought," she said, "that you might be able to give me some explanation."

I replied grumpily that I had never taken part in a whale hunt and, as far as I knew, there were no whales in our water. I repeated what I had already told the landlady, but Tsana would not be put off. "And what if they catch the whale?" she asked, and winked at me as if she were arranging a date. I was about to answer her curtly and tell her she wasn't to talk to me about whales, but my colleague, the bookkeeper, interrupted in time and remarked that our fishermen would never be able to catch a whale. "How on earth could we do anything like that? We are not English or Norwegian. We're always setting ourselves up as some sort of whale and we aren't even pike, which could at least frighten someone. Someday someone will net us and drag us to dry land like so many sticklebacks.

The discussion about the whale began to take on a political flavor. My colleague's face twisted wickedly, and I got up hurriedly and went into the corridor.

I lunched in the canteen. The food was poor and tasteless as usual, and I went home immediately afterward. I felt sour and wanted the landlady to waylay me so that I could air my views about that whale, but she wasn't to be seen. I lay down and fell asleep and, as when I sleep best, I dived into the warm seas like a dolphin. But a knock on the door awakened me and roused me from a very deep and pleasant sleep. "Are you sleeping?" asked the landlady from the other side of the door, though she was opening it already. I raised myself on my elbows and shouted at the top of my voice at the landlady, who, dressed in a black apron and looking like the snout of a giant whale, peeped in at me: "Go to the devil! You know I try to get some sleep at this time." "It's nothing. Forgive me," she excused herself. "I only wanted to tell you the latest news on the radio." They caught the whale this morning."

I must have been expecting her to tell me just that, else how explain my fury? "Get out! Get out!" I flared up. "Go to the devil, you and your whale!" I jumped up from the divan and picked up a cushion, but she withdrew at once and shut the door, while I threw the cushion in futile rage against the wall.

That was how my quarrel with the landlady began that day. I remained furious, and she became frightened and began to make excuses. "I'm leaving, I'm moving," I said, all the while regretting what I was saying, for I knew that I would not be able to find a better room; it seemed to me that that wretched whale was depriving me of the room that everyone envied me. So, actually, I did not say that very firmly, but conditionally and a good deal more mildly. "Listen," I said, "only mention that bloody whale just once more and I will leave at once, and the housing committee will allot you a whole family: drunken husband, brawling wife, and four small children."

She knew that mine was no empty threat and didn't dare contradict me. "Forgive me," was all she said. "I thought you were already awake; it is four o'clock. I thought it would interest you, like the others in the house. I hadn't the slightest idea that you had any reason to hate whales so. I won't mention them again...unless you beg me to. For I know that you will want to talk about them!"

She couldn't resist adding this, but in fact she didn't speak to me again about the whale, though I noticed that she was always whispering and talking with the other lodgers about it, loudly enough for me to hear what it was about, but all the same not loudly enough for me to follow what she was saying. She behaved coldly toward me, as if she were offended; whenever she could not avoid talking to me, there was always something mysterious and ambiguous in her words, and the questions that she asked me, or asked others in my presence, were framed to pique my curiosity and force me to ask her the latest news about the whale. She even began to listen to the radio news, setting the volume so that, even through the doors I could only guess what was being talked about, but could not follow the words. She was punishing me by arousing my curiosity and by ostracizing me from her conspiratorial circle. It even seemed to me that she devised a special conspiratorial language with word ciphers, which she used to the other lodgers when I passed through the hall, or when she passed the time of day with the neighbors when I was in my room. They were big, strong, black, and forceful words, always heavy, coarse, masculine nouns, signifying something huge, strong, and powerful, which reminded me of the whale, but I was able to ignore them and had comparative peace for a few days, though I felt like a stranger in the house and as though I were being boycotted and avoided like some outsider. I must, however, admit that I, too, used a certain amount of craft, which helped me to endure the pressure and to restrain my own curiosity: I bought two dailies, one weekly, and the local Split paper, and followed carefully, down to the minutest detail, everything in them about the whale. But, so that no one should know, I did this stealthily in the office when there was no one else in the room—whenever anyone came in, I slipped the papers into a drawer and stood up, closing the drawer with my stomach, and I never took them home.

It was there, in the weekly, the second day after my quarrel with the landlady, that I read the news of the capture of the whale. Under the headline

FIVE-HOUR STRUGGLE WITH SEA MONSTER

the pilot of the Harbor Board, one of the principal participants in the hunt, spoke of this event to the reporter:

"That morning I woke with the feeling that something unusual was going to happen that day. Nor was I mistaken. About nine o'clock in the morning a woman dashed into the harbor master's office full of excitement and told me that she had seen a gigantic fish near the shore. I rushed madly to the place. I saw the black shiny body of the colossus and at once concluded that this was the whale.

"I called a number of sailors, and the news spread quickly. In a few moments a large crowd collected. We surrounded the whale on the land and sea side, and I directed operations from a bollard. We encircled the monster with a ship's mooring hawser. But when we began to pull it shoreward, a militiaman who had just come on the scene fired a shot into the whale's head. This infuriated the monster, which waved its tail and broke the hawser. Then it swam off, swift as an arrow, toward the other side of the bay, leaving a dense coating of blood on the water, which reddened the surface of the sea for a wide area around.''

Then I read through a description of the five-hour struggle, in which the said pilot had particularly distinguished himself, and a detailed account of the difficulties that had to be overcome before the monster was pulled ashore, with the help of more than two hundred bystanders, assisted by two trucks, a boat, and a large crane. The description, which was really exciting and read very well, was illuminated by several photographs (the whale, the pilot, the militiaman, and other helpers). That witch Tsana, the typist, cut out the pictures and stuck them on the wall above her typewriter and read the article over so many times that she learned it by heart. The sickly bookkeeper began to drink cod-liver oil and his breath smelled of fish.

After that there was no more news about the whale for some days. There was an unexpected lull, and we existed for the most part on stale news and warmed-up comments. To keep the story alive, the press filled its columns with more accounts from the lips of new and additional "eyewitnesses."

The columns headed "Do You Know?" "Matters of Interest," and "From the Whole World" spoke of all kinds of whales: Greenland whales, belugas, Biscay whales, cachalots, bottlenose whales, humpback whales, sperm whales, pilot whales, rorquals, grampuses, narwhals, and Leviathan, of extinct varieties and the Loch Ness monster, of whales which had been seen in our waters over the past half-century, of the story of the huge whale backbone in the Vienna Museum, of the exploits of our whale hunters in northern seas and the whale hunters of Yugoslav origin in Tierra del Fuego. The economic section told of the great advantages that our industry could derive from this whale and calculated how many dinars it could save us. Then it went on to talk about ambergris, the expensive perfume base for which whales are mainly hunted, of whale oil and whale-bone, and put forward a proposal that our country should revive its whaling industry and build a fleet of whale-catchers. In the foreign political section, there was much talk about the internationalization of seaways and division of spheres of interest, and of the dispute between the great powers about the Arctic regions and of the International Whaling Conference which was to be held in Canada. The social section wrote about the brave sailors who, heedless of their own safety, took part in the capture of the whale and of the reward that ought to be divided among them. The magazine section published medieval descriptions and wonderful eyewitness accounts of Leviathan, and referred to Jonah, who was swallowed by a whale. A professor wrote a detailed article entitled, "Where Do the Whales in the Adriatic Come From?"; and there was a description of whales in literature; and the novel about the white whale, *Moby Dick,* was published in installments.

I also noted facts that had never till then occurred to me, how the word "whale" was in much more frequent use than I had ever thought; that other people, outside the circle of my acquaintances, were interested in whales, and that the whale was a much more important factor in our lives than I had ever suspected.

I kept hearing people, in the streets or in the office, talking at the top of their voices and mentioning the word "whale" or using it as a basis for various phrases, for example: "a whale of a time," "wailing winds," "Prince of Wales"; then there were words that recalled whales, such as: weal, wale, wail, walrus, and poetic words like waley. In the trolley-bus I heard them reprimanding a man who was trying to shove his way to the top of the queue: "Go easy there. Don't push like a whale!" And, in the street, a woman saying to her husband, who had turned to look at a pretty girl: "Why do you gape at her like a whale?" And, in a more favorable form, some mother chatting to an acquaintance in the park and saying of her son, a sturdy urchin, that he had grown "till he looks like a whale." In an old novel I read that "it was as dark as the inside of a whale," and, in a poem, more modern but less comprehensible:

"You rose out of the waters, raging and lewd as only a whale,
The great whale known as Mac, can be.
You were as you are, statuesque but filled with ire—
Beating headlong upon the walled-up threat of loyalty."

In the papers a sports reporter said about some boxer that he was strong and "had a punch like a whale," and the posters clamored: "Grownups and children, drink the medicinal fish oil WHALE! It restores youth and gives strength!" And even the sparrows in the streets seemed to be chirping it.

I, too, despite all my efforts to defend myself, trying to exclude the very thought of whale even from my subconscious, found myself forced ever more frequently to think or speak about it. I did so with the utmost distaste, as if, to me, it were guilty of something; as if, in the well-known phrase, it bore the mark of Cain. I hated the whale as a keen fisherman hates the big fish on his fellow-angler's line. I was irritated by people who spoke of it and hated those who spoke well of it. It gave me pleasure to learn that whales are dying out, and I would have had even greater pleasure had I learned that the very word had been erased from our vocabulary, since I could not wipe this race of outsized mammals from the face of the globe. But, nonetheless, I noticed with regret that even against my will the whale kept coming more and more into my thoughts and my life, destroying my peace and my mental balance. Though I concealed this even from myself, I realized that, slowly and surely, it continued to hold my interest, and then I even felt the need to begin a conversation about it, like a man with an uneasy conscience who inevitably begins a conversation about his wrong-doing. When others spoke of the whale, I desperately tried to remain silent, but I listened and went on listening—even though I tried to convince myself that the subject did not interest me. I could not overcome this tendency, though I knew that it was both silly and dangerous.

The other day there was a conversation in the office between the bookkeeper, Stanić, the cashier, Marković, and three or four colleagues from the nearby rooms and the floor above, a conversation just after ten o'clock, when one eats a bite and drinks black coffee. It soon turned to the whale. "Nothing new in the last few days," one of them complained. I kept silent, stubbornly silent, till I could stand it no longer and broke in, though still cautiously and in a roundabout way, with questions:

"Nothing new about what?"

"Oh, that beast. It's not a needle, to get lost."

"Who knows if it's really as big as that?"

"You saw it for yourself, in the papers."

"The papers! Why should they keep mum about it on purpose?"

A colleague from the floor above was already getting bored with the conversation when the troublemaker Tsana broke in—she had a lardy cake in her hand which she had just gone out to buy—and said at once from the doorway what I, too, I must admit, already knew but had intentionally said nothing about.

"But it's on show already! At Split, in the main square. Everyone's gone to look at it."

"That's really worth saving!"

"The crowds are enormous. They can hardly control them."

"Just like them! Hold up five fingers and they'll come to have a look."

"But I'd like to see it, too."

"Can you wait that long?"

"Why that long? It'll soon be here in Belgrade. Ten days in Split, a fortnight in Zagreb and Ljubljana, and then, it'll be here!"

She was quite right. It was all in the Split morning papers. Who could have pointed this out to her and how could she have had a moment to read them? I asked myself, suspecting she must have some secret, high connections, when the bookkeeper butted into the conversation, raging and furious. He was foaming at the mouth, as so often when the conversation turned to politics; he was a young official, but it gave him satisfaction to pose as an ardent and offended Serb.

"It's always the same," he said. "You're quite right. We Serbs are last every time. We'll even be the last to see the whale, when it will already be stinking. Why Zagreb and Ljubljana first? I ask you: Is Belgrade the capital or isn't it?"

That was the way it was for a week or two after the first news about the whale. As at election times when they give the results of the voting, there were daily reports in the newspapers that so many thousands of citizens had seen the whale in Split, and, during the first week at Zagreb, twice as many. I saw it several times in the movies, pictures of how they had managed to load it onto a train at Split and unload it at the Zagreb station. There were several broadcasts about it on the radio and accounts of the crowds and speeches. Then one day a huge blue whale, gaily waving its raised tail and spouting two magnificent clouds of vapor from its nostrils, appeared right in the middle of Terazije Square and swam, in the form of a neon advertisement, over a new bar called "The Blue Whale." In the hall at home, so hung that I couldn't help seeing it every time I opened the door, there was one page less on the wall calendar every day. Meticulously and industriously the landlady tore them off, as if she were numbering the days that still separated her from her meeting with the whale and as if she wanted to show me how short a time was left before its arrival, so that she could ask me: "Do whales exist, then? Are there any in our seas? Have they caught one and has one at last come to Belgrade? What have you to say about it now, Mister Lodger?"

What could I say? Nothing, when confronted with this ever more evident and striking proof. I would have to keep as mum as a fish, not to have to acknowledge my defeat.

On the eve of its arrival, I went to visit my married sister, who lived in Cvijic Street in one of those houses built just after the war with paper-thin walls, so that one could hear every word through them. My brother-in-law, an engineer, was not at home. My sister and I sat in the warm, pleasant room, chatting and gossiping, while her little daughter, ten, in the first grade of the elementary school, was lying on the floor drawing something. It was a long time since I had enjoyed such a pleasant domestic atmosphere, until someone in the next flat turned on the radio at full volume. They were listening to the news. In a special, raised voice, the speaker announced through the thin wall: "Here's is an important news item! I am able to inform all our listeners that tomorrow evening they will be able at long last to welcome in our town the great whale known as Big Mac!" He went on to say something more, but we couldn't hear what it was because several voices, young and old, broke in on the other side of the wall and shouted: "Hurrah! Hurrah!" Then they began dancing and jumping about, probably around the table, like cannibals around a cooking pot with a man in it. "Listen!" said my sister, raising her head from her sewing, and I could see that her eyes were shining with joy. Even the little girl raised her eyes from her drawing. She showed it to us. It was a whale! Something big and black, smudgy and crude, but undoubtedly a whale, with wide-open mouth, as if trying to swallow me. "Will you take me to see it?" she asked me, and at once demanded that I tell her a story about a whale. "Go on," said my sister. "I've told her all I know already, and you certainly know a great deal more."

What could I say? I felt myself betrayed, driven out of my own home, out of my own family. The whale seemed to have found its way even here and settled down. My former pleasant mood turned sour. I felt humiliated, I couldn't answer any of the child's questions, but got up and went out with my tail between my legs.

All the same, that evening I went to the public library and looked up everything that I could find about whales.

In the encyclopaedia was written:

"Whale (Cetacea), a sea mammal, sometimes of enormous size (up to 330,000 lbs.), of fish-like appearance, without hind limbs and with forelimbs in the form of fins; certain varieties have teeth, while others have large bony plates in place of teeth, which serve as food filters. Owing to excessive hunting, many species are in danger of becoming extinct. Whales live for the most part in cold seas and feed on tiny sea organisms. There are two main groups: the toothed whales (Odontoceti), which include the dolphin and the narwhale, and the toothless whales (Mysticeti), which include the Greenland whale."

That wasn't much. So I began to skim through other books as well, and found in a maritime textbook a history of whale hunting from its earliest beginnings down to our own times. There was a description of the various ways of whale hunting, data about the number of whales caught during recent years, the number and type of whalers, their nationality, the boundaries of the spheres of interest of the great powers in the North and South polar regions, and an extract from the International Conference for Whale Protection. I found out that a whale breathes with lungs, like land mammals, a thing I had not known before. It surfaces every three minutes, breathes in air, and then dives once more, but, when it is wounded, it may remain under water for as long as half an hour. It grows to as much as thirty yards in length and breeds in the usual way. The female whale bears young and suckles them. Whaling is very profitable, for all parts of the whale are valuable to industry. Even in the margarine we eat there are certain constituents taken from the body of the whale; the greatest number of perfumes are based on ambergris from its intestines; women's corsets are made from whalebone and luxury objects from its skin; its bones are ground into fish meal, which is used as cattle food and artificial fertilizer.

So, I thought to myself after reading all this, the whale is present everywhere; he can be found, directly or indirectly, in the food we eat and in many of our joys and pleasures, and he witnesses to a certain extent our most intimate pleasures. This led me to gloomy conclusions which did not give me much satisfaction.

I noted all this down industriously and was the last to leave the library, staying there until I was reminded that it was time to go. But, just the same, I couldn't manage to read everything and take notes—the literature about whales was so extensive! I decided to continue coming until I knew all that any living man could know about whales; at least more than anyone else in Belgrade, even including those who were most enthusiastic about them.

The evening papers, which I bought on my way home, described the arrival of the whale thus:

"Tomorrow the great whale, known as Big Mac, which was captured near Split six weeks ago and about which so much has been written in our newspapers, will arrive in Belgrade on the morning train from Zagreb. The whale has been on view at Split and Ljubljana, and more recently at Zagreb, where, according to our Zagreb correspondent, it aroused astonishment and interest. There is not a man, woman, or child in Zagreb who has not seen the whale, and there are many who have seen it several times. Even now, though its exhibition period at Zagreb had to be extended for longer than was originally intended because of the great interest shown and the continual crowds, the citizens are much grieved at its departure and have taken every advantage of their last chance to see it once more.

"The whale will have to be placed on a special truck because its transport to the railway station presents special difficulty. In view of the great and widely expressed interest of the people of Belgrade, the whale will, according to our information, be exhibited in Tas-Majdan Park every day from eight in the morning till eight in the evening, that is to say, twelve hours without a break. Entrance tickets will be very cheap, only twenty dinars for adults and half-price for children and soldiers. The entrances will be so arranged that there will not be a crush. So, people of Belgrade, the whale awaits you!''

There was little work done in the office that morning, and there were few who remained seated in their usual place. Everyone was filled with suppressed excitement and felt the need to move about continually. They paid interoffice visits, talked, and found excuses to go out of the room and lean over the first-floor balcony, to call out to one another from room to room or call one another up on the phone. Tsana tripped about as if she were younger by half her years and at least thirty pounds lighter; her breasts seemed to jump about from her blouse. My colleague, the bookkeeper, was continually breaking and resharpening his pencil, and the messengers burst into the room without knocking. I guessed from the conversation and the flushed, excited faces what it was all about, but no one said a word to me. They were far too excited and preoccupied to have time to talk to me, and too happy—like children—to want to tease and irritate me. They forgot all about me, and only that filly Tsana, telephoning, sat provocatively at my desk, but turned her back to me so that I could not hear the answers at the other end of the line. She continually referred to "him," avoiding any mention of "his" name. "I heard about him yesterday. I must see him. Let's all go and visit him. Who? Surely you know who. 'Him.' Surely I don't need to explain everything to you aloud. Isn't it interesting? I'm sure we'll have a fine time. Dress up well and warmly; I imagine we shall be out of doors for some time," and so on. Then she turned to me provocatively and roguishly and smiled, as if to show me that I wasn't the only pebble on the beach and that there were others who would, even if I wouldn't, to stir my curiosity and make me jealous.

But I felt neither one nor the other. I knew she was talking about the whale and I had no particular interest either in her or in him. She was too old for me, too plump and forward for my taste, and as for "him," quite simply I detested him. But still, I felt hurt by all this, like a child excluded from a game. The landlady's tactics were being repeated here too, though in a different way. Therefore, when old Bubalo, our filing clerk, who felt himself under an obligation to me because of some services I had once done for him, and wanted to return good for good, appeared from somewhere or other at the end of the working day and sat down opposite me on the other side of the desk and deliberately turned the conversation to the whale, trying to put me in a good mood, I shied like an unbroken horse and began to sulk. I was cross, as I always am when someone wants to talk me over and convince me, and I rebuffed him so roughly that I felt sorry for him when he got up and went away hurt.

I was irritable, since I guessed at once what he wanted; he had come to comfort and console me, thus letting me know that he thought I had lost the battle. He therefore sat beside me and began to fiddle with the papers on the desk, obviously unsure of himself and not knowing where to begin; it gave me a definite and cruel pleasure to let him go on tormenting himself, so I didn't move a finger to help him. He began to beat about the bush with, "How are you?," "What have you been doing?," and "I just came over for a little chat," and so forth, whereas I knew very well that for years old Bubalo had never risen from his seat in working hours save for the most urgent of reasons.

"Are you thinking of going to see the whale?" he asked at last, as though casually, after long hesitation. "It arrives in Belgrade tonight!"

"Well, everyone will be going to have a look at it. As for me, I thought it would be enough, having regard for my years, if I looked out of the window at it as it goes by. My legs are not very steady, and I am afraid to go into crowds. The comrades agree with me. What do you think? Would that be all right? They won't blame me afterward, will they?"

"That should be quite enough," I consoled him. "They won't blame you. Does it interest you so much?"

"Interest me—why not? It's a whale, after all!"

The old man drummed with his fingers on the desk and turned to look around the room, as if to be sure that no one was listening, though we two were quite alone there.

"But what have I to do with it, even if it is a whale?" I went on spitefully. The old devil within me drove me on.

"That means . . . ," he said almost sadly, turning his head away so as not to look me in the eye. "Then it means that it is true what they say, that you are against the whale."

"Against the whale?" It seemed silly to me. "Why should I be against the whale? Does it represent any political party, that I should be against it, or is it a human being? No, I simply have no attitude at all towards the whale. What does it matter to me? I have quite enough worries as it is, and have more urgent things to do than to concern myself with a carcass. What's the whale to me? For me, it just doesn't exist. It doesn't exist, and that's all there is to it! Do you understand?"

I got angry, raised my voice and even thumped my hand on the desk. But I felt that I was telling lies and that my vehemence showed this.

"Anyhow," I asked, outwardly calm again, "Who told you this nonsense that I hate the whale?"

"Well, it's not very pleasant for me to talk about it, and I don't want to get involved in any office intrigues. Everything, I am sure, was with the best intentions, and they didn't want to accuse you of anything. It was only some talk in the office this morning about the whale, and we all decided that our office would be one of the first, if possible, to pay it a visit. It was arranged for tomorrow afternoon. Then someone mentioned that you, too, should be told, and even put on the organizing committee; but Miss Tsana said that you had shown no interest in the whale, and that even now you didn't want to go and see it, for you...in fact...in fact...she said, our colleague Rade hates the whale! Then someone said that perhaps she had been mistaken—one mustn't make hasty judgments—and, if someone talked it over with you, it would be found that it was not so."

"That was you, Uncle Miloš!" I exclaimed, moved, and the old man hung his head still lower, and I knew that I had guessed right and that it had been he who had rushed to my defense. Poor old devil, I thought, with a feeling of gratitude and sympathy. He had been a civil servant for more than thirty years and could hardly be blamed if he were frightened and nervous of everything, even of the whale. It was fine and brave of him to decide to defend me.

"Thank you," I said to him, and felt that I should try to calm him and be sincere with him, though in fact I had not the slightest idea what to say. My whole relation with the whale was not clear even to me. (What rubbish! Had I gotten to the point of defining my attitude towards it?) I did not know whether I was perhaps really indifferent? Or was I, in the depths of my being deeply interested in it, but because it was the fashion and because everyone was talking about it I did not want to admit this even to myself? I hadn't thought enough about this, and it now seemed to me that I would have to clarify my views and come to a decision. Nonetheless, I took it on myself to say to the old man:

"I ask you, what is this that a man must either hate or love it? A bit of carrion! A dead fish! What does it matter if, for the sake of argument, I do hate it? Can anyone be blamed for that? Who cares? And who is any the worse if someone is interested in a whale, or someone else in the races? Are we all obliged to dress in the same fashion, and, if someone or other loses his head, must all the rest of us at least lose our hats? Our bookkeeper collects stamps and you, so I have heard, breed pigeons, so what harm can I do if I prefer something else to the whale—say, a beer?"

He was alarmed and looked about him warily as he rose, interrupting me. I felt that I had gone too far, said more than he could bear to hear. "That's all very well," he said on his way to the door, "but the real point is that just at this moment people are interested in the whale and it doesn't do to go against public opinion." He paused for a moment in the doorway and added sadly: "In any case, what is life except—to be an onlooker. I, as an old man, know that very well."

That was all he had to say to me. He obviously did not want to give his opinion about the whale. It was two o'clock, time to leave the office.

As I went to lunch through the side streets and then, later, in the canteen, sat sullenly at a table for four at the end of the somber room, bent over the stained and crumpled tablecloth, over the caraway soup and cold bubble and squeak, crumbling the stale bread and suddenly convinced that I was out of sorts, I thought over the morning's events and my conversation with old Miloš Bubalo. I consoled myself, like a child, that I didn't care what other people thought, that it was all the same to me what my colleagues at the office thought of me or the landlady or all the other damned fools. How does it concern me? I thought; what do they matter to me? Let them hate me! I have...and I couldn't recall what I had! What had I that would compensate for good-fellowship and friends. With what and for what could I live alone, without friends, and what had I that others should envy me? How had it come to this? Why and how had I become separated from the friends with whom I had up till now lived in harmony? How did it happen that I was at daggers drawn with my landlady, about whom, to tell the truth, I had no complaints? Damnèd whale! It was responsible for everything. But what harm had it done me that I should be so set against it? What had I against it?

I thought it over. As a man born on the coast and familiar with the sea, I had no reason to feel aversion toward any sea creature. I remembered that many of my ancestors had been seamen, but I had never heard that any of them had been harmed by a whale. As far as I knew from various tales, the whale is a quiet and gentle creature which never attacks unless it has been wounded. So, therefore, what did I have against the whale? For, I must confess, my feeling for it was one of bitterness and hatred. Was it perhaps a question of jealousy and envy, because it was now something of importance—the newspapers were writing about it and all Belgrade was interested in it—while I was nothing and no one, a little man, a civil servant, to whom not even the waiter in that bloody canteen would pay any attention?

My head spun with all these foolish thoughts, and, more hungry than satisfied, more melancholy than bad-tempered, I made my way home in the hope that, once shut up in my own room, I should plunge into my afternoon sleep, from which, I hoped, I should awake refreshed and in a better mood. But the landlady waylaid me in the hall. I was able to see from her flushed face that she was determined to spoil even that well-earned afternoon rest. To make it worse, I knew that in the mood I was then in and after my recent thoughts I should neither be able nor dare to stand up to her. So I hunched my shoulders and tried to get past her into my own room. But that was quite impossible! Arms akimbo, she was standing in the hall doorway and on her lips I read—whale!

She was determined to rub my nose in it, even at the risk of my actually giving up my room and sending her a family of seven. She looked like a woman who has for years been forced to keep silent to her husband and then, all of a sudden, has resolved to say everything and face him with it, come what may.

"Well," she said, "what have you to say for yourself now?"

"Good afternoon," I answered mildly.

"Have they caught it?" she went on, still without giving it a name. She was holding that back till later, till the decisive moment, but I knew that then she would not fail to use it. "Do you still insist on contradicting me? Haven't you anything to say to me?"

"Firstly: How are you? Then: I hope you are well. And lastly: I am tired today." I tried to wriggle out, but she would not let me.

"Are the papers lying, now, Mister Rade? Was I right or not? Does it exist or doesn't it?"

"What?" I asked foolishly, in order to gain time, so that I would not have to reply at random, but at once realized that I had made a mistake and had simply asked that the whale be thrown in my face.

But she still hesitated. "What? Who?" she repeated slyly. "It's I who ought to be asking you that. Who doesn't exist?" She paused for breath and sighed deeply, like a whale when it comes to the surface. For a moment there was a pause; I could hear the floor squeaking under my feet. I knew: now it will come, now everything will pour out, and in fact, I was not mistaken. She did not keep me waiting long.

" 'Who?' you ask me," she said, and peered into my face. "Who else, my good sir, but the whale, the whale, the whale! The big whale, known as Big Mac!"

What could I do? Carry out my threat and move at once? What would I gain from that when the whale had already, so to speak, one foot in Belgrade? And how carry it out in the mood I was then in, and with the thoughts that had been passing through my mind since noon? She, too, knew perfectly well that I would not be able to; she felt stronger now that the whale was approaching, so dangerously, so threateningly. But I couldn't put my tail between my legs like a whipped dog and crawl back into my kennel without a word. I must at least try to save my face, even if I could no longer save my prestige, and, therefore, I pretended not to understand and tried to make light of the whole affair.

"All right," I said. "What if they have dragged the carcass to Belgrade? I am tired and I want to sleep."

"Ah, so now you want to wriggle out of it," she said, stopping me and holding on to my coat. "Now it doesn't matter, but, before, you threatened to give notice if I even mentioned it. You didn't even want to believe the papers, and now, when we've succeeded in bringing it here, now, when we who believed in it have shown you that it does exist, now you would like to get away with a 'so what?' While I was fighting for it, you were jeering at it; and now you would like to get away with a 'so what?' While I was fighting for it, you were jeering at it; and now, you think, it's no matter! Wait a bit, wait a bit! You won't get away with that!. . ." She tried to hold me back, but I managed to find a favorable moment to slip past her to my room, and, just as I was at the door and felt safer, I couldn't resist giving vent to my spite and shouting at her:

"What do you mean by all this? Why are you so taken up with it? It's not yours. You didn't give birth to it, even if it does look like you."

She flared up. She screamed. But I quickly closed and locked my door and threw myself panting on the divan. I was quivering. With teeth clenched and stiff all over, I tried not to let a sound escape me. So this was what I had been driven to! Everything had happened quite naturally, one thing leading to another, everything was so intertwined and went along of its own volition, as if there could be no other way. The landlady began dialing telephone numbers, calling up all her friends. She shouted into the receiver so that I, too, would be able to hear what she was saying, and she talked, of course, about the whale: how its arrival was an unusual event, how this was a unique chance to see something so unusual, and who knows whether we should ever get another such chance. "You see," she said, "if I had died yesterday, I could never have seen the whale (no, nothing has happened to me, I'm just supposing). And there are people who don't appreciate it. That's what our people are like. They envy anyone who is superior and more important than they are. It seems to me that if any honor is paid to anyone else they take it as a personal insult."

She went on speaking in this way with a second and a third acquaintance, described the whale, estimated its length and weight as if she had caught it herself, and as if she (and not I) had been born by the sea and as if her family (and not mine) had been concerned with fishing, and as if she had spent her whole life whaling, whereas

I was convinced that she had never even been to the seaside, that she didn't even know how to swim, and that carp and catfish were the only fish she had ever seen. But that didn't prevent her from using anglers' terms and from inviting all her women friends to join her in a visit to the whale. "They must let me see it," she asserted. "I fought for it when other people didn't even acknowledge its existence, and I have quarreled with the lodgers who were against it," and she again began to abuse me. I waited for her to hang up, seized my opportunity, slipped into the hall, and fled into the street.

I didn't know what to do with myself. I felt homeless, like a student who hasn't been able to find a room, and that incited me to wander aimlessly and to go for a stroll in Kalemegdan Park. In any case, I always spend my spare time so stupidly, never do anything for myself, that I did not know when I last had had a breath of fresh air, under the open sky and with open spaces around me. I go to the office at seven, and spend my time after lunch sleeping, and then, now and again, look in on a friend or go to see Desa when her husband is not in town, on the quiet, naturally, and then go somewhere or other with her and then—back to my wallow. I work overtime on the balances to earn a bit more, for it is not easy to live on one's pay. Then there are trade-union and National Front meetings, visits to my sister, and various other social chores. So, there you are, one is always in a hurry and a flurry, as if one were always hurrying across the street so as not to get run over. Time flies. And for time past, ever since I turned forty, it seemed to slip away even faster.

By good luck, it was a fine day. Sunny but cold, with a touch of frost. There was no one on the streets, and everything was so cushioned and silent that I had to keep walking so as not to fall dozing on a seat. I went to the outer bastion of the fortress and looked out to where the two rivers join. The water was high, for the snows had begun to melt. The Sava was the darker and the Danube the lighter. A boat, just out of winter anchorage, was steaming along towing after it on a long steel hawser three broad black barges, like three huge captured whales. They looked just as dead as they rode over the wake left by the steamer. I couldn't bear to look at them.

I turned aside and, in a few moments, found myself in front of the gates of the Zoo. What had I been searching for then, the last time I had been here, in summer, with my little niece? And what, I asked myself, was I searching for now, in winter and alone? It was suddenly clear to me that I had not wandered here by chance, for no reason at all. Consciously or unconsciously, my hatred and my spite had led me here; I had come to visit the lions, panthers, tigers, leopards, lynxes, jackals, wolves, bears, and all the other beasts to whom, when the dance was over and the enthusiasm had died down, as in a circus, I would throw the whale. I licked my lips and enjoyed, in advance, my feelings; I would like to see those muscular, supple animal bodies, those powerful jaws and white teeth tear, rend, break it into pieces and gnaw it, powerless and at their mercy. I was almost horrified at the cruelty of my thoughts. But, nonetheless, for the last time on that accursed day, I tried to do something. I raised my hand to open the gates.

The gates were shut. A keeper was collecting the litter left behind by the small children.

"Are you shut, Comrade?"

"Yes."

"Why? Because it is winter?"

"All the others have gone to look at the whale."

"The whale?" I said in wonder. "But what do they want to do that for? Surely it's not alive?"

"No. But, all the same, it is a beast. We ought to be on hand when it arrives."

An elderly man in a dark-blue uniform and peaked cap, he went on picking up the paper and paid no further heed to me. With dragging footsteps, I went back into the Kalemegdan. But there in the park there was no longer anything pretty or pleasant. The sun had gone down and everything was once more winter cold, twilight, unpleasant. Not a man in sight and only a flock of ravens against the blue-gray sky. A loudspeaker, hidden somewhere in the bushes, began to blare. A commentary on the whale! I heard the hoarse tinny voice from its throat and the sound of the tinsel circus music, the hum of the crowds, and I hurried to get away.

On my way back, nearer the Terazije, I met more people, who, as though in expectation of some great event, had been unable to loll at home and were walking about the streets. I looked in at the apartments of two of my friends, but found no one at home—they, too, had gone out to seek relief from this inner uneasiness and great impatience. I couldn't call on Desa, so what could I do? I sat for some time in a café, and then, when it was quite dark, overcome by my worries and in a state bordering on tears, wanting to get drunk and to cry my eyes out, I went home, rejected, outcast, foreign and alone in my own city.

And all because of the whale. Because of him, Big Mac, whom everyone was admiring, to whom everyone was devoted, and whom tonight, through the darkness, by the light of torches and the smoke of lighted newspapers, they would bring in triumph from the station, bound with ropes and riding in his carriage, like a new divine, pagan idol and great juggernaut, fat and black.

Darkness was all around. All the town seemed asleep. And only the solitary, cold, bitter, and awake yellow-eyed light of my room stared intently at the dark until late into the night.

* * *

I don't know how I staggered home or what happened then. The next day when I woke I found myself in my bed. I was weak, as after an illness, a heavy drinking bout, or a severe hangover. I opened the window that I had sealed up, since in any case it was no longer of any use as a shield, and it seemed to me that the air was a little clearer and less laden with stench. Perhaps there had been a wind last night? It has saved us, I thought, and at once my servile, civil-servant conscience awoke. I got dressed and set out for the office.

I was one of the first to arrive, if not the only one on the first floor. Then I remembered that today was the fifteenth; I was due to report to the assistant director. So at all events I went to his office, not expecting to find him there. There were no secretaries in the anteroom but, when I knocked and peeped into his room, I saw him there in his usual place at his desk. He motioned me to come in and offered me a seat. He was fresh and well-groomed, clean-shaven, and immaculately dressed, smiling, as if nothing had happened. There were flowers in the room, and a fan whirred softly on a filing cabinet, making the room still more pleasant.

"Good morning, Comrade Despić. Always hard working and conscientious. This morning, you are certainly one of the first."

We chatted for a little. I said that I had seen no profit from my conscientiousness, and then, taking a deep breath, I told him that from today, the fifteenth, that is, on the prescribed date, I must submit my resignation. It was, unfortunately, under the circumstances, impossible for me to remain any longer, and I had already found a job in another office, in the Communal Bank. It did not seem to make any special impression on him, and that almost hurt me.

"You know, Despić," he said calmly, playing with a paper knife, "I foresaw this, and it comes as no surprise to me. In fact, I myself warned you of it in good time. So I will not try to induce you to stay, though I know that I am losing my best employee. In any case, I am sure that, with your capabilities, you will find a good position, such as you deserve. The director of the Communal Bank is a good friend of mine, and I will have a word with him."

That was all he said to me. He was neither cordial nor unpleasant. He was correct but not intimate, though I knew I was closer to him than any of the other employees. It was not in his nature to become confidential or to show his feelings. He was a real gentleman.

Nonetheless, when I rose to leave, he saw me to the door and in order to show me some sign of partiality on my departure, he said, offering me his hand:

"You know, in confidence and for your ears alone, we were really in great and serious danger. They did not know what to do with that enormous rotting whale. There were no means of transport available; and the general situation yesterday evening was very serious, even critical. But the street cleaners saved the day. By their own action. By their everyday methods, with shovels and brooms, they saved the city last night."

He gripped my hand and closed the door after me. I went down to the first floor and came upon some of my colleagues who had arrived at the office. I greeted them coldly and sat down in my place. I worked. About noon the assistant director strolled through the room, but didn't seem to notice me. He went up to Tsana, who was once more muttering to Uncle Miloš about the whale and its backbone, leaned over her papers, and said, unusually loudly and severely: "Listen, Tsana, pay more attention to your work! There are more important things than whales!"—and went out.

I realized that he had said that for my benefit. That was all he could do, since he, as a gentlemen, could not intervene in the quarrel. But to me it meant something even more; I knew from that moment that it was really all over with the whale.

* * *

And so in fact it was. But for all that, there was still talk for some time to come about the whale. Since no one knew what had happened to it, what it had been used for, or where it had ended, one could hear citizens grumbling that, in fact, the oil smelled of whale, that shoes or soap stank of it, and there were even some who said that the milk had a sort of unpleasant, fishy taste. When they wanted to say (in guarded terms) that someone was seriously ill, or that he would lose his job, or that he was suspected of some irregularity or theft, they would say of him that he "smelled of whale."

I was already working at the Communal Bank. The director received me amiably. "I have the very best reports of your work," he said, and then added, looking a little askance at me, "Only it seems to me that you are a little ..." and stopped there, as if not knowing how to go on. "Anyhow," he concluded, "I don't think you'll have any occasion, here with us, for squabbles."

In fact, I have been working there for three months and feel quite content. Firstly, I am at peace and therefore I feel content. I rarely see my former colleagues. Since my office is in a different district, I have also changed the canteen where I have lunch, and, whenever I come across any of them by chance, we do not know what to talk about. I don't hate them, but it seems to me that they do not like me. I remind them of their sinful past, and no man likes that.

I no longer speak about the whale, though now and again I feel a desire to do so, like some old warrior from the Salonika front who recalls with great pleasure his wartime memories. But I know that I would bore people, and therefore I refrain. But still, one day in early summer, I walked slowly, dragging my steps, to the Tas-Majdan. I felt a little nostalgic and wanted to revive old memories. The smell was no longer there, and, when I got nearer, I was astonished to see everything changed. Where the high wooden wall and the field had once been, there was now a deep pit, the foundation for some great building, which seemed to me like a deep, enormous grave for the whale. I tried to find out about it, but there was no one who could tell me anything. The people began to look at me strangely, and I thought the better of it.

They took it away one night, secretly and in the darkness, with the greatest speed and without ceremony and honors. They took it away without a catafalque, without mourners, and without witnesses. The filthy job was entrusted to the street cleaners, and they cleaned everything away with their brooms and shovels and threw it into the sewers, onto the city rubbish dump, and into the rivers, which wash away everything and carry it downstream. In their haste they did not even manage to preserve the backbone, and so our state museum remains without even this trophy which would have borne witness to the whale's visit to our city and would have been an attraction for foreign tourists. In other countries and cities they would have acted otherwise, as is proved by the backbones and skeletons to be found in them.

With these sad thoughts and tired from my walk and dazed by the sun, I made my way home. I walked calmly into my room, took off my coat and shoes, and lay down on the divan to sleep. I was in my first, best, sleep when I was awakened by a loud conversation in the next room and the door of my room being gently opened.

"Are you asleep?" asked the landlady, peeping in and then coming into the room. Still drowsy from my first sleep I jumped up with head muzzy, not knowing exactly where I was or what had happened, and, holding my falling trousers with both hands, I shouted: "What is it, for God's sake? Not something more about a whale? What has happened now?"

She did not seem to notice my confusion. She was in her best silk dress and her best summer straw hat, with handbag and gloves in her hand, all ready to go out.

"Won't you come to the movies to see *One Day of Life?*" she asked. "It's the saddest film in the world! Everyone's gone mad about it. All Belgrade is going to see it, and now the whole city is weeping."

"I will not!" I shouted angrily, and the blood rushed to my head. "I will not go to see it," I yelled, even though I, too, was quite ready to weep. I threw myself down on my bed and turned my back to her.

I knew it; there you are, a new whale! I remembered my peaceful job in the bank. I was conscious that once again I had made a mistake, that once again I was vainly in revolt against something that it was not needful for me to resist or to get wrought up about.

But—I could not help doing so!

Translated by Lovett F. Edwards

BRANKO ĆOPIĆ

(b. 1915)

Ćopić was born in the Bosnian village of Hašani. He received his education in Banjaluka and at the University of Belgrade. During World War II, he fought on the side of the partisans. Since the war, Ćopić has lived in Belgrade as a professional writer.

Ćopić is a prolific writer of short stories, novels, poems, and plays. He is often satirical about the contemporary situation of his country. He is one of the most popular Yugoslav writers today, especially among children.

His works of distinction are: *Breakthrough* (1952), *Adventures of Nikoletina Bursać* (1955), and *Gunpowder* (1957).

Ćopić's most important contribution to contemporary Yugoslav literature is his initiation of post-war Yugoslav satire. His satire is simple, direct, and to the point.

In the satirical short story, "The Election of Comrade Sokrat," Ćopić achieves an entertaining exposure of the local bureaucrats. There is an easy transition from the real to the imaginary, from the amusing to the problematic. The range of Ćopić's humor is wide—there is broad laughter, sarcasm, parody, and a strong sense of mockery.

What gives his stories their particular flavor is their language. They were written in what is sometimes described as modern "folk tale." That is, they are told in the first person by their semi-literate "hero" in a weird and often hilarious mixture of peasant idiom and the ill-digested concepts and jargon of the new society.

The Election
of Comrade Sokrat

THE HUNTING LODGE "The First Hit" was completely full. The Association of Hunters was holding its yearly meeting. The large hall was embellished with current signs: "Long Live Hunting!" "Let's compete in hunting for a better life!" "You are worth as many horns as you have."

Although all present in the hall were bound by one and the same passion, hunting, they were divided into two different groups: hunter-comrades and simple hunters.

The hunter-comrades were, as a rule, the higher government officials known by their excellent guns and other equipment procured abroad. For them, the hunt was "arranged" in advance: the beaters and the assistant hunters shot at the wild animals at the same time as the hunter-comrades to assure that the shot of the comrades would be as accurate as possible. They talked about the boars and ducks from nearby estates, which the comrades caught and were paid for afterwards from a special fund for the advancement of hunting.

The "simple hunters" were our various domestic hunters; they were left over from the old Yugoslavia. Nobody paid particular attention to them; it was not known when they would start hunting, nor when they would return. During the meetings and gatherings of the hunters, the hunter-comrades would try wholeheartedly to educate politically the simple hunters and to point out to them the importance of hunting for our economy. Nothing helped. The simple hunters talked skillfully about rabbits, foxes, and dogs, but the political and economic side of the question they neglected as if it did not exist.

On this particular day, the elections for the new officers of the hunting organization were to be held. The old officers enthusiastically saw to it that the elections would be prepared, so that no unguided elements from the old school would prevail. Ten or so members were found and seated strategically among the members so that they would "spontaneously" nominate the new candidates. Thus, full democracy was assured in the elections everybody talked of.

When the elections started, the president asked if there were a nomination. One of the "spontaneous" members shouted, "I nominate comrade Bošković." Since comrade Bošković was one of the most distinguished hunter-comrades responsible for the ideological re-education of the hunters, everyone in the hall roared, "He accepts!"

"If you please, who has a nomination for our next officer?" said the president.

One of the "spontaneous" asked to be recognized again and suggested another candidate previously approved by the old committee.

When the assembly was electing the fifth or sixth member of the new committee, suddenly a little, haughty old man from the last row asked to be recognized.

"I propose comrade Sokrat because of his long hunting activity!" stated the old man.

The assembled hunters were momentarily confused and started murmuring. No one knew Sokrat, and they did not know what to do.

"Who is it?" asked a husky hunter.

"Surely some important comrade," whispered his neighbor.

"You know how it goes, perhaps a directive came from above to select this comrade," explained the other hunter.

"That is so, I swear to God," agreed the people around him.

Behind the president's table, there was confusion. Comrade Sokrat was not supposed to be elected; no one from the old committee knew him. Finally, the president of the committee shrugged his shoulders in bewilderment and asked, "Does Comrade Sokrat accept?"

"He accepts," roared the entire hall.

"Does anyone oppose?" added the president, making a last attempt to spoil the election of the unexpected candidate.

"There is none, none," answered the hunters, and, somewhere in the corner, one of the members candidly winked to his neighbor, "Watch the president provoke us. He thinks someone stupid will oppose, so he can report his name. Well, we are not going to do it. Even if we are only simple hunters, we still remember who Comrade Sokrat is."

"Well, then, is my candidate accepted without a single vote of opposition?" asked the old man.

"He is accepted, of course, he is," replied the president.

When the elections were completed, the president of the committee asked the newly elected committee to take its place at the president's table.

With abounding applause from all the members, the new members started walking towards the wide table of the president. The last one walking was the little old man, along with a dog.

A former president, having seen him walking the dog right to the president's table, yelled, "Hey, where are you going with that dog?"

"Well, he is also a new member of the committee," explained the old man with an air of importance.

"What new member?" asked the bewildered former president.

"This is Comrade Sokrat, whom I nominated," proudly answered the little old man. "This is a famous hunting dog."

"Well, how can a dog be a member of the committee?" started protesting some of the members.

"Well, you elected him unanimously," proudly insisted the old man. "Did I not nominate Comrade Sokrat? I did. Did you accept him? You did. What then?"

There was a murmur among the hunters, many started approving.

The little old man is right. We elected it. We should have thought about it earlier and asked questions.

"Well, how can a dog be right?" asked one of the hunters.

"Well, of course, my young friends," said the old man in a fatherly way, "my Sokrat was elected in a fair democratic way; the elections are valid."

"That is true," replied a number of the members.

"It is not so," stubbornly insisted one hunter, till one of his friends, after carefully looking around, approached him and whispered in his ear, "Shut up, you stupid man. What do you know who Sokrat is, and who sent him? It seems to you that that is a dog, and who knows who it may be? You know—it may be a conspiracy."

The man opened his mouth wide, and then nodded his head in approval. Then he shouted as loudly as he could, "Long Live Sokrat!"

So Comrade Sokrat became a member of the committee of hunters, and, since nobody knew who sent him there, everybody was very kind to him, patting him and approving of him.

There is a rumor that Comrade Sokrat gives useful and smart proposals during the meetings.

Translated by Branko Mikasinovich

JOŽA HORVAT
(b. 1915)

Born in Kotoriba, Horvat started writing before the Second World War; his works of that period emphasized a didactic type of literature, with simple but effective language. After the war, he wrote plays with light irony and humor. His plays, *A Finger Before Nose* (1948) and *Sold Consciousnesses* (1956), brought him literary esteem.

Horvat's novel, *A Cat with a Helmet* (1962), one of his best achievements, is a humorous and satirical presentation of the war period. In a confused war situation, a partisan by the name of Kapara was wounded fighting the Germans. In his dream, Kapara found himself in a small village, Mousehole. Kapara was a captive of a strange group of united guerilla fighters of opposing ideologies and interests—Ustashe, Domobrans, and Partisans. As a partisan, Kapara finds it difficult to understand a scheme devised by the villagers to protect their population in wartime.

Mousehole

(An excerpt from the novel A Cat with a Helmet)

WHEN A MAN IS HIT on the head with a rifle butt, all kinds of things rush into his mind, while other things rush out. An unbelievable, but true discovery: Partisans, Ustashe, and Domobrans are living together like turtle doves in love and harmony in the village of Mousehole. These are tactics and strategy of the village leader, who has never been to a military academy. Will Kapara agree to shoot wild duck instead of Domobrans, Ustashe, and Germans? Face to face with the vast steel hulk of a tank, what did he do to save his life when there was nothing else he could do? . . .

Kapara opened his eyes with difficulty. He was lying in a bed in a strange room, fully dressed, covered with a light eiderdown. There were pictures of saints on the walls, pictures of unknown people, a bride and groom in their wedding clothes, old men with moustaches, children in white. . . . Through the window he could see willows and part of a murky river flowing lazily and sleepily by. Frogs croaking, some birds singing. Where was he? He closed his eyes again to try to think how he could come to be here and where in fact he was. Had he been wounded, captured—what had happened to him? The sound of voices reached him as though in a dream. "Has he come round?" "No." He opened his eyes just enough to see who was so concerned about him, who was talking.

Through his eyelashes in the half light he made out an Ustasha! He was leaning against the window sill and looking towards the bed, looking at Kapara! The Ustashe emblem—a bomb and the letter "U"—could be clearly distinguished on the yellowish-brown uniform. There could be no doubt about it, Kapara had fallen into the hands of his deadly enemies! What now? Where had it happened? When? How? But before he could think of anything, another shadow moved and stopped by the window. He opened his eyes a fraction—and gasped! A Partisan soldier was now standing beside the Ustasha! Two caps, a red star beside the fizzing bomb! An Ustasha and a Partisan! They were standing side by side looking at Kapara. "I must be dead," he thought. "I am dead or I've gone out of my head! What's happening to me, where am I?" He closed his eyes to try to think more clearly, but, wherever he began, however hard he racked his brains, he could not for the life of him remember when and how he had come there. Or was he perhaps in a fever, seeing things, and that vision of the Partisan or an Ustasha did not really exist, was it all a mirage, an hallucination, a dream? To make sure, he opened his eyes once again, opened them wide this time, but there was no longer either a Partisan or an Ustasha by the window. Sun, the trailing branches of willows, and the murky water barely trickling along the river bed. What had happened to him? Where was he? "Where am I? Where am I?" he cried aloud, his voice trembling with fear and uncertainty, and a voice from beside his pillow replied: "Thank God...have you come round?"

Kapara recognized the voice. The Domobran! Yes, that must be his voice! Delighted, he called him: "Franjo!...Franjo!...

"Here I am, here I am?"

The Domobran ran up, put his hand on Kapara's forehead and asked anxiously:

"You're alive, then?"

He tried to turn his head, but it hurt him. "Franjo, where are we?"

"In my house."

"In *your* house?"

"That's right...in Mousehole. You know, you wanted to come here."

"Mousehole? What's that?"

"You know.... I told you about it.... It's my village, the one my sister wrote that the war was over in."

"The war is over...?" Kapara was dumbfounded, he sat up and opened his eyes wide. "The war is over? Then what am I doing here?!"

"Calm down, Kapara, the war is over, but it isn't over. It's only in our village.... Lie down, don't move.... Lie quietly!"

He did not lie down. He stared open-mouthed at the Domobran, not believing his ears. Frogs croaking, birds singing...

"And how did I get here? What happened to me?"

The Domobran asked compassionately:

"Don't you remember anything, Kapara?"

"No."

"Can you have forgotten how we met up in that barn that night, and how we killed an Ustasha early the next morning?"

"Yes...yes...I remember! I took the knife to him while you held his legs to stop him struggling. And then what happened?"

"Do you remember how we gave the Ustashe the slip, got out into the yard and ran through the garden and the orchard till we got to that little wood, to that canteen?..."

"Yes, I remember that as well."

"Just before sunset we reached a shack in a vineyard, where we rested, had something to eat and drink, slept the night and set off again the next morning. We walked for hours and hours without stopping until you got fed up. You said that you had done enough walking in this war and you didn't want to go any further when there were so many cars racing along the roads. I begged you not to do anything stupid, but you ordered me to be quiet and set out straight for the main road."

"No, I don't remember that," admitted Kapara truthfully.

"You don't? We reached the wide asphalt highway and the first person to come along with a legionary, you shot, took his revolver and rifle, kept the revolver and gave me the rifle. We dragged the body into a ditch, and then you put your arm around my neck and ordered me to hold you up and take you to the middle of the road. So I did as I was told, and you began to limp as though you had been wounded in the leg. And we walked and walked like that until a car suddenly appeared. You waved to the driver to stop;

the brakes screeched and the car drew to a halt. Do you remember that?''

"No, I don't. What happened next?" Ilija was worried.

"Next? Well, all sorts of things happened and I was driven yet again to curse the day I met you. So, seeing you limping along like that, the driver stopped the car, and two soldiers got out and came towards us, presumably to see what had happened to us. And as they were coming towards us a third soldier got out of the car, a giant—a German, with a rifle in his hand! It was too late to run for it. You raised your pistol, and, while you were killing the first two, the third one, the German, rushed up and hit you on the head with the butt-end of his rifle, but he hit you so hard that you immediately collapsed and lost consciousness. Seeing that everything was going so badly, I aimed my rifle hastily at the giant and shot him.''

"You killed the German?" asked Kapara in a tone of disbelief, but the Domobran was adamant.

"Yes, I did. I killed him and then I threatened to kill the driver too, if he so much as moved and tried to escape. Somehow, we dragged you into the car and I sat beside the driver and showed him where to go. Just before we got to Mousehole I told him to stop. We pulled you out, I went to the village for help, and we brought you by cart to my house. And here you are, under my roof.''

"And is that all?" asked Kapara.

"All? Do you want more?"

He did not reply at once. He was thinking about what the Domobran had said, and he could not get over his amazement at having forgotten it all. Or was it because he had been hit on the head?

"When did it happen?"

"Three days ago. If you hadn't had a helmet, your skull would have cracked open like a hazel-nut in a squirrel's teeth. The squire came to see you the day we brought you in.''

"Squire? What squire?"

"The Squire, our squire...you know our village, our landlord. He's got an inn and a shop. A very able man. He's our organizer and, as we soldiers would say, our strategist! He never went to military school, but he manages to arrange everything...wisely and cunningly! He knows everything and understands everything. A politician!''

Kapara frowned. Something deep down warned him to be on his guard. "An able man...landlord...strategist...politician...." These were all words that meant a lot to a Partisan, he smelled a rat, and Kapara had good reason to frown. He had heard various things about these village philosophers and peacemakers and had met some of them here and there and argued with them. And that is why he now asked cautiously:

"And this general of yours came to see *me*, a corporal?"

"Yes, he came as soon as he heard what had happened. You were lying here like this and he came to your bedside, looked at you for a while and said: 'If he doesn't kick the bucket soon, he'll live a long time and not be any the worse for this!' And then he added: 'Let me know when he opens his eyes and when he can stand up.' I'm on duty, I make you hot and cold poultices alternately, and wait for you to come round. And here you are, conscious again, thank God!"

He was worried: what did the squire want from him?—Let him know as soon as I can stand? I shall certainly call on him as soon as possible. Let's reassure the fellow, in a moment he will see before him Ilija Kapara, Partisan warrior. What an interesting meeting that will be!

"And why do you keep making me these hot and cold poultices, Franjo?"

"Because I was scared stiff. I wasn't sure which was better for you, hot or cold compresses, and I was terrified in case you died on me! People could have thought I poisoned you or got rid of you in some other way. How could I have proved my innocence to your mates in the brigade? A Domobran would rather die than try to explain the truth to a Partisan. That's why I nursed you as best I could, and now that you've opened your eyes there's a weight off my mind. You once saved my life, Kapara, and I am happy to have been able to repay you somehow."

Kapara briefly reviewed his "saved life" and said, without particular enthusiasm: "Thanks!"

"There's nothing to thank me for. How are you feeling?"

Yes, how am I feeling? wondered Kapara bitterly. Perhaps it would have been better if he were dead, if that German had finished him off on the road, perhaps that really would have been best. And he must have hit his head mighty hard, as he could not remember anything at all. Bloodily...he tried to turn his head—and succeeded! He did feel a dull pain in the back of his head, but, since he had heard all that had happened to him, that pain was not even worth mentioning. He tried to turn his head again. No problem. All was well! Then he stretched his toes to make sure that he could move his joints. He was satisfied. Kapara knows—as long as a Partisan's head and feet are all right, there is no need to worry about anything else.

"Do your bones creak?"

"Where?"

"In your head."

"No, nothing creaks."

The Domobran looked carefully at Kapara and noted with satisfaction. "Well, you certainly are quite a fellow! Anyone who goes anywhere with you had better take at least three spare heads; I never believed I would make it to the village alive with you, but, whenever we've been in a spot together, I've seen that you are a really crafty old fox and that there aren't many like you. If I had to travel through the world again, on the run, a deserter or a fugitive, I would always go with you."

He was not listening to the Domobran. His thoughts were circling round the picture that had caught his attention when he had opened his eyes a short time before: the Ustasha and the Partisan side by side leaning on the window sill!...Had he been awake or dreaming?

"No, you weren't dreaming," explained the Domobran. "That was my cousin Torban and his son."

"Your cousin is an Ustasha?" Kapara was alarmed.

"An Ustasha?...He's not an Ustasha. Well, he is, but only sort of...."

"And his son? Is he a Partisan...only sort of?"

"Of course. We are all Ustashe and Partisans and Domobrans, but no one is really either an Ustasha or a Partisan or a Domobran. We are only sort of...."

"Sort of what? How?"

"Simple. All the men in the village have been divided into three groups—Partisans, Ustashe, and Domobrans. Everyone has his own uniform and spends a month in each group."

"What! A month as a Partisan?!" exclaimed the astounded

Kapara, quite unable to grasp this remarkable system.

"That's right."

"And then?" gasped Kapara. "What happens then?"

"You change! All those who were Partisans become Domobrans, Domobrans become Ustashe, and Ustashe Partisans. And so on, in turn, because no one wants to be an Ustasha before the time comes, people are frightened. And to avoid a few people suffering for the whole village, we take turns."

"I don't understand," said Kapara. "How do you mean—so that a few don't suffer...suffer what?"

The Domobran was a little confused. But then thought of something. "Well, because we're armed. We're protecting the village."

"From whom?"

"From everyone."

"And?"

"What?"

"If soldiers come, do you fight?"

"My goodness, you are slow!" said the Domobran amazed. "Why, that's just how we've been so clever!"

"How?"

"Because we don't fight. We are for everyone! We are for whichever army comes to the village."

"If Ustashe come?" Kapara was studying the Domobran carefully out of the corner of his eye, but the latter continued to answer calmly and reasonably.

"If Ustashe come, they are met by our Ustashe. What else?"

"When your turn comes, you'll put on an Ustashe uniform?"

"Of course." The Domobran was astonished that Kapara could not understand. "I've already explained that it's all just for show....We are all Partisans and Ustashe and Domobrans, it's all mixed up here. The Squire decides each month and organizes the shifts...and you take what you get."

Kapara found himself becoming gradually but uncontrollably angry. He stared furiously at the Domobran. He would have liked to hit him, but he restrained himself, somehow, and went on quietly.

"And what's your duty?"

The Domobran blinked and sat down on the bed beside Kapara

to sort out his ideas. This Partisan corpse had scarcely opened his eyes and come partially back to life, and here he was bombarding him with questions, examining him like a criminal on trial, tormenting him and worrying him. Now what did he want explained—duties?

"Our duty...our most important duty is not to join any side. Not Tito's or Pavelić's. None outside our own village! To stay at home, look for ourselves, keep quiet and save our skins, that's our first undertaking, our main slogan, and our only one! The Squire says—'When the war is over we shall see who is left alive and what will happen.' For the moment our motto is: 'Wait and save your skin!' "

So that's it, thought Kapara. That's your great strategist Squire's policy! Let others fight, let others perish for freedom, and he will sit tight in Mousehole until the war is over! The wretch! Kapara had known about all these lordly dodgers for a long time; he knew all the infamous ways of village peacemakers like this one, who slumber beneath the skirts of the occupiers like badgers and long for only one thing: that there should be as few partisans as possible, that the fascists should kill as many of them as possible, so that on the day of liberation they can poke their noses out of their lairs and snatch the power from those who fought for freedom! Kapara knew all this, but still, seeing that he was in the pigsty, he wanted to hear and learn as much as he could.

"So that's how it is, you say.... The Squire decrees the shifts and you suffer!...It's quite fair, a month at a time for everyone! And what happens when soldiers come to the village?"

The Domobran answered readily: "It doesn't happen very often. Our village is cut off from the rest of the world. There is a river running round it and impenetrable forests all around. It's really very rare that an army calls on us."

"All right, it doesn't often happen," Kapara granted. "But, nevertheless, if it does sometimes occur that a group of soldiers gets lost and wanders even into this Mousehole of yours, what happens then?"

"You'll see, when you recover a little.... In the middle of the village there's a high firemen's tower. It is manned day and night by a watchman who keeps a lookout, and, as soon as he catches sight of approaching soldiers, he rings the bells, and that's the signal for alarm."

"And then what? Do you grab your guns?"

"Oh, no! First we listen carefully to the bells. Because we've got a special signal for Ustashe, a different one for Partisan, a third for Domobrans, and a fourth for Germans. . . . The whole village listens, and, according to which army it is, some stay in the village and others run for it."

"Ah, so some people do run after all!" Kapara was relieved.

"Well, yes. . ." Franjo affirmed, "some run. No one absolutely trusts anyone else. Someone has a relation in the real Partisans or the real Ustashe, and everyone watches carefully to see who's coming. The only person who never stirs from the village is the Squire. He meets all the soldiers and sees them off. His door is wide open to all commands and all officers. The other people who always stay here are the men on duty."

"You have men on duty as well, do you? Well, I never!" Kapara was genuinely surprised.

"On duty. . . I don't mean duty officers like in the army, but Mousehole duty officers, Domobrans or whatever, depending on which army is coming. If it is a Domobran division, then the Domobran shift is on duty in the village, and so on. They're like landlords, if you like."

"And what do these landlords of yours do when they're on duty?"

"They meet the army. . . . My goodness, Kapara, you sound as if you'd never been a soldier! They are on duty in order to meet the army and, when they come, whoever they are, they go out to meet them and ask them what they want: whether they would just like to rest a little or whether they intend to stay for a longer period; whether they would like something to drink, to quench their thirst, a light snack or a hearty meal. If they only want a little rest, the men on duty offer them shade in orchards, barns, farmyards. If they want to stay the night, they get rooms and beds. If they want to drink, they are offered wine, brandy, beer. If they want a snack, they are given spare ribs, green paprika, and yogurt. If they are hungry and want a good meal, then they are offered goose, duck, turkey, chicken, fresh fish, dried fish, wild duck, sausage, proscuito, dry chops, cheese, butter, cream, eggs, drippings, calves, a heifer, a cow. They are given anything they ask for."

Kapara shook his head sadly: How nice!. . ."

"Why, yes, it is. . . . That's our contribution to the struggle. We look after them, stock them up, feed them, and, when they've had enough, we accompany them to the edge of the village, making sure they don't steal anything on the way."

"That, too!"

"Yes, of course, soldiers steal!"

Kapara closed his eyes. . . . Oh, Ilija, where the hell have you got yourself! All around you are liars, squires, and hawkers, frogs croaking, murky rivers flowing, and where are the Domobrans and guns, where is your brigade, where are your mates, where is Kalnik—you slob?! Get up, whatever are you sitting for!

Kapara lowered his feet to the floor and tried to stand. He staggered but the Domobran held him, helped him, and Kapara stood upright. He tightened his belt, buttoned his shirt, pulled on his boots, and asked where his helmet was. His helmet was in the cupboard, and, when the Domobran took it out and showed it to him, Kapara was able for the first time to assess the blow that had laid him out. The thick steel had a deep dent about ten centimeters long in it. The Domobran remarked confidingly:

"If he had hit an ox, it would have been curtains!"

"For whom—the ox, me, or the Germans?"

"The ox! But your head is so hard that you could drop a tree on it without ill effect."

Kapara did not reply. He tried to straighten the helmet as best he could, placed it slowly and carefully on his head, and then turned to the Domobran.

"Where is my rifle?"

"What do you want it for?"

"I need it."

The Domobran took the rifle out of the cupboard and gave it to Kapara. He opened it and pushed a bullet into the barrel.

"Let's go!"

"Where?" asked the Domobran, nonplussed.

"To the Squire!"

"The Squire?"

"You told me he had been here and that he wanted to see me."

"Yes, I did...." the Domobran was confused. "I did, but there's no need for you to go rushing straight off there now. There's plenty of time. The main thing is that you are risen from the dead, and there's lots of time for the living. Lie down!"

"I don't want to. I want to see the Squire. Show me the way!"

The Domobran could see that Kapara was angry and that no good could come of this unexpected meeting with the Squire, and that is why he tried to persuade Kapara to postpone the visit for the time being, but to no avail. He had no alternative but to follow Kapara outside. When they were in the street outside the house, Ilija stopped and looked around to see what this famous village looked like. There was an endless row of one-story houses along the bank of the river which encircled the village like a horseshoe. Woods stretched away into the distance on the far side of the river: willows, poplars, acacia, and reeds. Fat grey gulls were circling over the river catching fish and squealing quarrelsomely. There were water lilies near the bank. Here and there, fishing nets. Frogs croaking. A whole flotilla of slim, black boats was rocking sleepily in the shallow water nearby.

"What do you need so many boats for?"

"The Squire had them made."

"Who for?"

"For us. I told you, as soon as any soldiers come, some of the villagers run away. They jump into the boats which are always ready, push themselves off, cross the river, and then disappear into the woods and undergrowth. There is a lot of quicksand on the other side of the river and, if you don't know the way, you get sucked down without a trace. That's why no one chases the ones who run away. They are too frightened. The boats save us!"

"And the Squire thought all this out?"

"Everything!"

"What a wise man!"

"Very wise. You'll see him in a minute."

Kapara pointed to the tower which rose up in the middle of the village. "Is that your tower?"

"Yes, that's right. His house is right beside it. He's got an inn and a shop."

"A shop...what kind?"

"Oh, he sells everything. Needles, petrol, shoes, scythes, yeast, handkerchiefs, flour, matches, tobacco, postage stamps, buttons...everything! He feeds and clothes half the village. We are all in his debt. But the Squire is a good man, he says, 'Just take it, you'll pay when the war is over!'"

He's a good man, all right...the skunk! Kapara made a face and added: He'll pay and all!

They passed the fire tower and stopped in front of the largest house in the village, a huge one-story building, the façade of which was divided into two parts. Over one door was the sign "The Inn of the Happy Hunter" and over the other "General Stores—Anton Squire." The landlord received them in the inn. He could have been fifty and weighed twice that in kilos. He was wearing a shirt with the sleeves rolled up; he was hairy, red-faced, greasy—a real Squire. Seeing Kapara, he waved cheerily:

"Hello, soldier! Have you recovered? As soon as I saw you, I said, 'The likes of him are not going to get killed by rifle butts. Mortar fire—only mortar fire! That, or the gallows. Anything else is a toy.' How are you?" He held out his huge brawny hand and went on gaily, reaching for a bottle of brandy: "People returning from the other world must first have a drink of brandy, good, strong, double-distilled brandy, to wash away everything that is not of this world. If everyone on earth lived in the kind of friendship that exists between soldiers and brandy, there would never be any wars. Drink up!.... Your good health, soldier!"

They drank. The three of them sat down at a table, then Squire frowned and began:

"Well?"

"Well, what?" asked Ilija naïvely.

"Are you staying?"

"He's staying; why shouldn't he stay?" The Domobran butted in. "That's why we've come, to make the arrangements. Isn't that right?..."

But Squire interrupted: "Quiet! I wasn't talking to you. Well?..."

Kazara did not reply immediately. It was not easy for him to reply when he did not know himself which way to turn. Whether to go to Zagreb, to go back to Kalnik, to cross the Sava and go to look for his brother in the Kozara mountains?

"I asked you a question. . . ."

"I don't know how to get across the Sava. I'd like to make it to Kozara; my brother is commander of a brigade there, and I'd like to join him. But I don't know how to get across the river."

"That's your problem!" Squire frowned harder and began to drum his fingers on the table. "I'm only interested in one thing: do you or do you not wish to stay here?"

Trying to find a way out, Kapara replied cautiously: "I'm not from your village. . . ."

"I don't give a damn!" replied the Squire.

"Absolutely," the Domobran broke in again. "The main thing is that you're one of us. It doesn't matter where you come from or where you are going. If you're for peace, live with us as long as you like."

"At least until I'm stronger," added Kapara, but he was thinking: I really should have slit this Domobran's throat in that barn; it wouldn't have been any loss. . . . "Yes, until I'm stronger," he repeated.

"Until you're stronger, or weaker, I don't mind. If you like, you can stay here until the end of the war. Only you must remember—there's no such thing as popular rule here. I do the ruling, I, Anton Squire!"

"I know," muttered Kapara gloomily.

"If you want to stay here, you'll have to abide by my laws, the village laws. Do what you like—during the day you can walk in the fields or fish, there are pike and sheath fish in the river; at night you can sleep or try your luck with the girls, play cards, sing, enjoy yourself—live, do whatever you feel like—there is just one thing I forbid you: you must not harm anyone. There's no war here. I've had the greatest difficulty in making our village secure, but now I'll answer with my life if anyone touches any soldier of any allegiance whatsoever who comes into my village. I'll answer with my life for any of my followers, but I insist on obedience and peace from everyone!"

Kapara twisted on his chair, scratched his chin, straightened his helmet, and then calmed down, leaned on the barrel of his rifle and looked intently at Squire:

"So...it's peace?"

"Yes, peace to all."

"Peace to the Ustashe?"

"Them, too."

"Peace to the Germans?"

"And them."

"And what do we do about everything the fascists are burning all over the country?"

Squire replied readily, decisively, and without hesitation: "That's none of your business! Has my village been burned? No. Has anyone from my village been killed here, at home? No. It's true that some people have died because they did not want to listen to me but went off somewhere "to fight for justice!" Thanks to my policy, no one has lost a hair from his head in my village. If you like the sound of such a policy, stay; if not, no one's standing in your way."

Slowly and cautiously, Kapara offered resistance:

"If all of us think of saving our own skins, who's going to drive out the occupiers and liberate the country?"

"Not you and I in any case! Not fifty Partisan brigades, nor a hundred! The liberation of the country is other people's business. The Big Powers! The English, Americans, Russians will worry about getting the Germans out of our country, and we, weak as we are, we must just cover our heads or crawl into a badger's lair and wait for the storm to pass."

Kapara straightened his helmet. He felt that the battle was about to begin, and he instinctively tightened the belt of his trousers.

"Right, then! If I have understood correctly, the Americans, Russians and English can die for us, and we just creep into a badger's lair and wait. Yes, that's nice, that's very nice...." Kapara agreed and then inquired cunningly: "And then, what will we have waited for?"

"When?" asked Squire, not seeing what he was getting at.

"When the war is over," explained Kapara.

"What for? You'll be alive! What more do you want?"

"Right...and then, what then?"

"Peace! There'll be peace!"

Kapara shook his head doubtfully: "I'm not so sure, I'm not sure.... I can't help thinking that the people who clamor for peace now, in wartime, will be the very ones to start a war when peace comes."

He stared at Kapara with his sharp little eyes as though he could not understand the point of what he was saying:

"All I'm saying is that I guarantee that you will stay alive, and you, what are you talking about? I've told you: we'll see what happens when the war is over."

Kapara frowned and nodded significantly: "Ah, yes...you will see, and I know now! If all the Partisans take your advice, throw away their guns and hide themselves away in places like Mousehole, if the people's army ceases to exist, then, when the war is over, our dear King Peter Karadjordević II will calmly return, and, with him, our dear police agents, our dear district governers, revenue officers, tax collectors, notaries—and what is more to the point our dear Draža Mihajlović and our dear Chetniks will return, and the first thing they will want to know will be, "Where are you, Kapara? Damn your eyes, show up so that we can slit your throat, you lousy Croat, you filthy Ustasha, you filthy Austro-Hungarian, where are you?" And thanks to you, there won't be any Partisans to protect me, and what then? Beat Kapara up, slaughter the poor systematically, and the Croatian and Serbian gentlemen will get along together again and share the power! So that's what you are proposing I should wait to see?"

Well, not even Squire, the great village wise man and strategist, had expected such a torrent from a Partisan corporal. He gaped at Kapara, flushed with fury, opened his mouth so wide that his little pig's eyes almost disappeared, brought his fist down on the table and thundered:

"That's enough! I refuse to go on talking to you! I've seen your sort before. You all trot out what you've heard from your commanders. Now you talk about the occupying forces, and tomorrow you'll be destroying God and private ownership. You'll be taking each other's wives and living like pigs. I've nothing more to say to you. Just answer: do you want to stay in the village or don't you?"

"I don't!" Kapara said angrily.

"Then get out, this minute! I don't want to see you for another second, get out of the village immediately!"

"I can't do it immediately. Wait until I'm a bit steadier on my feet. Don't worry, I won't stay."

"I've told you you can stay as long as you like, a day, a year, or to the end of the war, I don't care; but as long as you are in this village, you are obliged to obey my laws. For the last time—are you going to obey them or not?"

Seething with hatred, Kapara stared under his helmet at this fat monster of a Squire; but what could he do, where could he go, when he could scarcely stand upright? If he could only stay here a day or two to regain his strength and be fit to undertake the journey. What should he answer, what?

"Well?"

"We'll see...," said Kapara sadly, bowing his head. "I'll think about it all."

The Domobran patted him on the shoulder in a friendly way and encouraged him. "Don't you think about anything, but just make up your mind to stay here."

"No, no, I can't...I must think. I can't do anything like this. If you let me walk around a bit, to clear my head...."

Squire stood up from his chair, knocked back another brandy and agreed good-naturedly: "All right...so be it! Go for a walk and think. The countryside round here is lovely, you'll see. If you're a hunter, or if you have shooting and killing in your blood, then take a double-barreled hunting rifle and kill some wild duck, hunt foxes, snipe, deer—shoot to your heart's content!"

He went out and set off into the fields. Absorbed in his thoughts he did not notice where he was going or how much time had passed since he left the village. As he walked along a path between rows of ripe maize, he suddenly heard the sound of an engine! And not only one—a whole motorized convoy was moving along somewhere nearby. The thought that the enemy was somewhere near him filled him completely. He forgot the Squire and Mousehole and his pro-mises and obligation—everything! He took his gun from his shoulder and crept silently forward. At one point he looked round to see how far he had come from the village, but there was no sign of it or the firemen's tower. And the engines went on humming, ir-ritating his ears and nostrils. Like a wild animal stalking its prey, Karpara lowered himself to the ground and continued on his hands and knees, protected by the leaves and stalks of the maize. He was getting nearer and nearer to the place where his heart was dragging him irresistibly—to the enemy! That is the way it is: Whatever the cat whelps hunts mice, whatever the forest rears chases fascists! Just one or two more steps and he must see them, he could already see the clouds of dust billowing in the wind. They must be somewhere here, he must see them any minute now! He was right. At the end of the plantation the view opened out in front of him, and Kapara caught sight of the road. It stretched out silver in all the green, straight as a ruler, almost within arm's reach. Motor bikes were moving along it in two columns, and between them raced trucks, tanks, heavy artillery!... The soldiers had helmets, rifles on their shoulders, mackintoshes streaked with various colors—Germans! They were going at a steady pace, their eyes on the the road ahead. Withdraw—would you, you bastards, you would run! Kapara grasped his rifle more firmly. He could scarcely wait for the end of the convoy. At the end rode a solitary soldier, as if protected. Kapara took aim, followed the cycle for about ten meters with his rifle, as a hunter follows an animal on the run, and fired. The rifle cracked, the soldier let go of the handle bars, slumped forward and careered with his cycle into the ditch.

He returned to the village as fast as he could, the Squire met him outside the inn.

"Well, how do you like the country?"

"Very much, of course!" Kapara admitted sincerely. "I never dreamed you had such wonderful surroundings. Meadows, willows, the river—it's really wonderful!"

Squire understood what these words meant and smiled triumphantly: "So, you're staying?"

"I'm staying! I'm staying, but on condition that I can go off like this every morning and every evening, with my gun on my shoulder, to walk in this beautiful countryside and fresh air. I need it, it's like a tonic!"

"Quite right, Kapara, quite right...." approved the Squire. "I knew you would stay. You'll like it, you'll stay with us till the end of the war, you'll see. Come in and have a drink...."

And they went in. The Squire took the bottle to treat his new follower, the late Partisan Ilija Kapara, but, just as he was raising his glass, the bells rang out from the tower. Squire listened attentively.

"What is it?" asked Kapara, himself alarmed.

"They're ringing strangely, I don't understand the signal."

He ran out into the street, Kapara after him. At that moment a grenade whistled over the village and exploded. Rifle fire, mortar shells. Cries for help, panic, and a crowd by the boats. Germans were pouring in from all directions, between the houses, across the gardens. Motorcyclists, tanks, trucks, heavy guns....Smoke belched out and the whole village was suddenly enveloped in flame. Kapara took out his gun, ran into the inn and rushed through the kitchen out into the yard, but there, in the yard, as though it had been waiting especially for Kapara, a great monster of a tank was bearing straight down on him! The barrel of the gun was pointing straight at Kapara's chest and the engine was roaring so that the ground shook. Ilija could see there was no way out. He could not run, nor could he destroy the great steel hulk that was cutting off his retreat. He had no bomb, no petrol, and no bottle—what could he do, nothing! He stood helplessly facing the jaws of death and waited for his last hour to come. Must he die, must he really die? Crazed with fear and despair, he grabbed the tank gun with both arms and shoved it with all his force back into the tank. Kapara succeeded in thrusting the barrel right back into the tank, but the crew realized it and drove it out once more into Kapara's chest. Kapara pushed it away from him, turned it in all directions, but the luckless fellow felt his strength failing, he saw his fate, there was no avoiding it. Once more, with his last shred of strength, he turned the gun, and turned not only the gun but the whole tank, and as he turned it over he kicked its steel backside...

...and then he woke up. He woke up sweating and struggling. It was dark, where was he? A smell of damp, a smell of grapes, grape skins, must, wine....Was that someone breathing beside him? He felt around him...the Domobran! Yes, it was Franjo, the Domobran! And he remembered everything. The flight, the vineyard keeper's hut! The wonderful escape, the Zagorje vineyard hut! He jumped up, and shouted at the top of his voice: "I'm alive...I'm still alive!!!"

Translated by Celia Williams

DOBRICA ĆOSIĆ

(b. 1921)

A partisan fighter during World War II, Ćosić was born in Velika Drenova. Following the war, Ćosić had a brief career as a politician, but soon became a professional writer. His notoriety began with his first novel *Far is the Sun* (1951), and the work remains a classic of the occupation and resistance. His other novels are *Roots* (1954), *Divisions* (1961), and *The Time of Death* (1972), acclaimed as one of the masterpieces of the post-war Serbian literature.

Fairy Tale (1961), a collection of short stories, shows him ready to experiment successfully with satire and parody. His development as a satirical writer paralleled his ideological evolution. Becoming less political and more ideological, he was able to present a satire of trenchant originality: fear of supervisors, hypocrisy, and malicious attitude—all emerge with chilling clarity in the story "Freedom."

Freedom

THE FREEST PEOPLE of my generation become spectators and witnesses at trials. The Satanoid world, infuriated by its lack of freedom and happiness, is preparing for Total War against our freedom and happiness. By means of the sad, the stupid, the shy, the timid, the feeble and the naïve, and by means of fanatics, misanthropes, homosexuals, pessimists, lyricists, metaphysicians, Utopians, ascetics, masochists, all enemies of civilization and high technical standards, and other subnormal types, the Satanoid states are organizing a network of spies to ferret out all kinds of dissatisfaction and discontent with happiness and freedom; they are organizing acts of sabotage against our happiness, conspiracies against Him and Kamonia. Newspapers and books, radio and television, psychovision and somnovision, cinemas and theatres, music and painting, architecture and technology, restaurants and churches, museums and beaches, sports-grounds and shops— everywhere and without ceasing men are taught how to be happy and how to enjoy freedom, and warned against Satanoid aims and ideas and against Antiistic actions and methods. And yet there are more and more Antiists; they keep turning up everywhere.

The Forum of the Creators of the Future has told us that this is in fact a clear sign of the death agony of the Satanoid world, which is making a last desperate effort to destroy our happiness and freedom which are, of course, indestructible. In addition, they say, the appearance of so many Antiists is evidence the Kamonia, together with Him, is marching invincibly forward into a perfect future; and that this is the final, great purification of the Kamonian people of all kinds of weaklings, paranoids, cowards, unbelievers, and malefactors. In this last, sacred reckoning we shall commit to the flames the last remnants of doubt in our happiness; we shall confess all unfree actions, ideas, and intentions, and we shall punish once and for all every criminal and wrongdoer.

Our science and our art have shown us that in fact we are none of us entirely free from guilt in this respect; if we are not Antiist ourselves, we have certainly heard, or seen an Antiist, and we can be sure that on that occasion he did not let slip the opportunity cunningly and skillfully to implant his seeds in our souls; if we are not guilty now, there is a strong possibility that we will be; if we have not yet seen, heard, or met a Satanoid or an Antiist, there is every likelihood that we will do so. We are beginning to believe that every Kamonian is guilty, or that he could be or will be; if we have not yet participated in Antiist activities, we can be certain that we are present and future participants; to put it plainly, no one can be certain that one day he will not begin to have doubts about his happiness for one reason or another. So it is absolutely necessary for Him to continue to convince us of our Happiness and Freedom, that we should study His Principles more and more thoroughly, that we should love Him still more and convince ourselves of the fact that we could be even happier.

Every day and from all parts of the country we write messages of love and devotion. A movement is developing for the writing of such messages at the end of each day's work, after performances in theaters and cinemas, after concerts and football matches, after every joyful experience—such as the awakening of spring in the countryside, walks by the river, delight in the first snow, weddings, nights of love, the birth of a child, and, of course, after funerals. We must be continually expressing our love for Him, affirming the strength of our happiness and expressing gratitude for it, and bearing witness to our faith. To ensure the prompt dispatch of telegrams, the Post Office is opening special counters in shops, in all public institutions, in restaurants, factories, offices, and cemeteries, and we are promised that in the near future every house will have a special post and telegraph center for sending letters and telegrams to Him. In addition, teams of special advisers are being organized, consisting for the most part of poets, who provide those citizens with less literary ability and philosophic vision with new, pithy metaphors, lofty phrases, and eloquent epithets; this service is free. We are the creators of Total Love for Him: never in the history of the world has any people so greatly loved someone as we love Him.

We know by heart everything He has ever said; we study His Dreams, we speak with His Accent, we have all practiced His Gestures to perfection, we tell only His Jokes. Everything that He thinks, we all think, too; what He wishes we all wish; we all eat whatever He eats. Beetrage and Chocoroon, His favorite dishes, are always to be found in all restaurants; the Mariblack, His favorite flower, can be seen in every house in Kamonia; Pline, His favorite tree, has the place of honor in parks and gardens, and special care and attention is given to it; all citizens of Kamonia carry reproductions of His favorite fishes in their pockets and handbags; if we feel like having a good laugh, we listen to gramophone records of His Jokes. At those times when He likes pornographic pictures, all the existing textbooks and readers are replaced by new ones with the appropriate pornographic pictures, and grown-ups devote themselves in their free time to the philosophy and aesthetics of sex. The songs which He likes have become our hymns; in fact, we always recognize as a hymn a song which He likes best. Since He is, perhaps, a man of small or short stature, or will be such, or has been, or so it seems to us—for we see Him only in photographs—we must, just in case, be shorter than He; indeed, the harmony and unity of Kamonia is being perfected according to this truth: we elect to the Electory people of shorter stature than He; as short as possible, in fact, so that in all photographs where He appears with the Creators of Total Victory and other appropriate persons, He is not only a head taller, but unequivocally a giant among dwarfs. Our film stars, girl models, famous sportsmen and all other prominent people are shorter than He is; thus the Kamonian type of masculine beauty is a short man. The Cult of the Short Man is supported by fables and other historical literature. The Academy of Memoristics has published several scientific works, with lavish illustrations and exhaustive documentation, which confirm the fact that all great men and geniuses in the past were people of small or short stature. The Academy of Memoristics has also published an Anthology of Faults and Imperfections, which shows unmistakably that tall people in Kamonia are suspected of being Satanoids; from their early childhood tall people are subject to scorn and rigid control so that there is no possibility of them falling into Antiism.

In our total identification with Him, our freedom is conditioned by His allergy to meat. How to abstain from meat is one of Kamonia's major problems. The movement against eating meat has achieved massive dimensions and resulted in a general emasculation which is acquiring an increasing aesthetic significance, although it is not reflected so favorably in sporting results, especially in boxing and field athletics—not that anyone doubts for a moment that the spirit is stronger than the flesh. Another national problem is His short period of sleep and His most original dodecaphonic wheezing and snoring during His sleep. Although the Mass Non-Sleep Movement has yielded exceptional results—the national record-breakers sleep for only ten minutes—the snoring contests broadcast by the Central Somnovision Authorities have not proved so satisfactory: the whole of Kamonia is convinced that His snoring is musically unique and inimitable.

In addition to our Universal Happiness Contests organized at the beginnings of each season of the year, and the election of the Happiest Kamonian, our greatest glory is the Day of the Future. No one knows exactly when this day will be, nor why it is that particular day; the date is kept as a great secret. I suppose this is to prevent the Satanoids and Antiists from attempting anything that might spoil our Happiness. Of course, weather conditions also play an important part in the determination of the Day of the Future. It is always a fine day, with a gentle breeze. Indeed, as we never know which day is going to be the Day of the Future, not only are we always psychologically prepared for this celebration; we have even abolished the usual seasons of the year, and divided it up into Preparations for the Day of the Future and Analysis of our Happiness after the Day of the Future.

The general discontent with our lot in Kamonia is exclusively concerned with the inadequacy of our means for expressing our Balance of Happiness. The numerical indications of our National Contests for Happiness and the Enjoyment of Freedom have long ceased to satisfy anyone in Kamonia. The Academy of Joy has been asked to find a new and better method of calculating happiness, and the corresponding measures and equivalents in which we could at least approximately define our condition. Attempts to express tears of joys in tones, to measure laughter on the dials of an anemometer, pleasurable excitement in terms of gravitational pull and pure happiness in time units whose basic and lowest unit is the decens, have not, according to general opinion, so far yielded appropriate results. Moreover, the election of the Happiest Kamonian and the solemn proclamation of the victor have found many critics who have no doubt influenced his reputation. The imperfections of our criteria for selecting the Happiest Kamonian are well known to those of us who are volunteer Joysters who, together with the professional Protectors, go round the whole town and all its houses in turn for twenty-four hours on the Day of the Future; wherever the singing is dying down, the laughter becoming uncertain or hollow, or the party spirit losing its boisterous tempo, we supply appropriate remedies to revive the mood of festivity and rejoicing, which lasts for the time necessary for the earth to turn round on its axis. And so that the victors of happiness and enjoyment may not doubt the possibility of being even happier, that those who are Happiest of All may not become demoralized, He has proclaimed the Two Silent Principles: Happiness is eternal, subject only to one condition; and Light cannot exist without darkness, which exists from time immemorial.

After the Day of the Future we are happy that it has been and begin to prepare for the next one, continuing to vie with one another in our visions of Absolute Happiness after Total Victory. The rewards for an absolute vision not only ensure the glorious winners a place in history, but also give them the right to indulge in a brief mood of lyrical sadness when the autumn days come along. This liberty makes them exceptional among our free citizens.

But there are always more and more Antiists, and in places where no one would dream of finding them. Announcements of new Antiist conspiracies are published in the newspaper; one such serious plot was revealed in the Forum of the Creators of the Future itself, among the people closest to Him, people whom we had adored because they have become famous in happiness by loving Him and by freedom in the struggle against the Satanoids and Antiists. Ex-

perience continually confirms His revelation that we are all actual
or potential Antiists. This has called forth a new wave of gratitude
and admiration for Him.

Day and night the Protectors indefatigably seize and arrest Antiists; columns of Protectors' cars and ubimobiles from all parts of
Kamonia rush to the Defensories and fill them with criminals. Actually, the Protectors only fulfill certain technical functions, since
all citizens are in fact Protectors; every free and happy Kamonian is
a Protector as a matter of course, keeping a constant watch over
happiness for the sake of happiness. From midnight, onwards, in
front of the Protectors' offices, there are queues of free citizens
who have come to report Antiists and all those who do not believe
in or who doubt their Freedom; innumerable telephone lines have
been made available for reporting to the Protectors: in addition, a
special corps of volunteer Protector-Investigators is being formed,
and they attend a short course of evening classes on the recognition
of Antiism and Methods of Overcoming Silence. The gramophone-
record industry has made recordings of the General Principles of
the Theory and Practice of Suspicious Persons. These records are
in very great demand; every family wishes to possess them. In every
house people listen to and study the Science of Discovering Plots
and the Recognition of Antiist agents. For two hours each day the
radio broadcasts instructions and practical advice for the discovery
of Antiism; television and psychovision are also utilized for this
purpose, while the Guilty Men Quiz arouses such widespread interest that all trade and communications are brought to a standstill.

The country suffers from the lack of a sufficient number of
courts and buildings where Antiists can be prepared for trial.
Schools, hospitals and warehouses are converted into temporary
detention centers, while restaurants, bookshops, fashion salons, art
galleries, cinema and similar buildings are adapted for use as
courts. But even these measures are inadequate to meet the growing
needs. The Forum of the Creators of History has given orders that
prefabricated courts, designated by serial numbers like railway
wagons and shops of the river networks, are to be erected day and
night in all markets, parks, and public squares. The complex
numbers of these courts do not represent any technical trick, nor
any attempt to conceal Kamonian secrets from foreign, Satanoid
spies; these numbers, which include all the letters of the alphabet

and six-figure combinations, simply reflect the true situation with regard to the growing shortage of court premises.

My brigade of spectators and witnesses works in two shifts; and soon every court will pass sentence in three shifts. I attend the hearings from one o'clock in the morning until midday! I have no time for breakfast. In short pauses, while the criminals are led in and out, we are given instructions as to how we should give evidence and how we should behave towards the criminal. Moreover, even we ordinary spectators and witnesses put forward creative suggestions for the rationalization of sentencing. While working on the night shift, which is mainly devoted to passing judgment on dead offenders who have been denounced and vilified by living Antiists, I, as a free citizen, feel some uneasiness that the triumph of liberty and right is not absolutely complete; so I wrote a letter to the newspaper TATATA suggesting that, in the cases concerning dead Antiists, the usual bureaucratic formalities for sentences "in absentia" should be dispensed with and the sentencing of volunteer criminals be introduced. These would be happy citizens of Kamonia who would volunteer to represent the dead men, i.e., to play the part of the guilty men and receive their punishment. Such volunteers should be chosen at special and illustrious assemblies from among the freest and happiest citizens; lists of these honorary criminals should be at the courts' disposal and as soon as required, they could be summoned by telephone and sentenced just like guilty men. Naturally, it would be better if they received their accusations in good time, so that they could prepare exhaustive confessions, but as this would present technical difficulties, and much time would be lost in summoning and bringing them to court, the simplest thing would be to have a certain number of volunteer criminals in reserve in the Defensories prepared for all crimes.

My proposal was received with enthusiastic approval by the free public, and one of the Creators of the Future greeted my initiative in His name, paying full tribute to it. There began to develop a movement of "Voluntary Criminals" whose numbers, and readiness to accept all punishments, especially the death penalty, amazed even our most loyal subjects.

I became famous overnight. Both the daily papers and the illustrated weeklies were full of my photographs, my biography, my achievements and anecdotes about me. I have been elected Rector of the Corps of Spectators. I have been proposed for the Electory, since, in addition to my services to the cause of Liberty, I fulfill all the other conditions required for the highest legislative and political body of the land. I have a strong voice, which is essential for the prolonged and loud chanting in the Electory whenever we look at His photograph, or at someone who is thought to have seen Him at some time, or who is likely to see Him before He dies. As well as a strong voice, I have remarkably large and muscular hands, which are essential for applause in the Electory, and also an excellent nervous system and the inborn patience required for sitting without moving day and night while listening to His program for the Perfect Future and the Plan for Total Victory, which members of the Forum of the Creators of History take in turn to read. But I have begged to be excused from election, because, as a young spectator at the courts, I feel I have not yet acquired the experience necessary for a politician. This modesty of mine has caused some of my colleagues to have doubts about my Freedom. I just set my teeth and say nothing, convinced that I am so happy that everybody else will soon be convinced of it. So I just get on with my work, freer than ever before, but just in case, whenever I have a little time to spare, I call in at the Center for Righteous Feeling Design or the Self-Service for Accepted Facts.

Meanwhile the criminals confess their crimes, and make some contribution to the accusation according to their intelligence and feeling for historical perspective. Many of them beg for the death penalty, and these we spectators greet with free and prolonged applause. The court carefully defends the criminals, diminishes the weight of their confession, and gently announces the penalty which is always milder than the criminals themselves wish, or than they ask for.

The cases concerning the suicide of parents, children, neighbors, and acquaintances are even more interesting than these classic ones. In this former type, in addition to establishing the fact of the suicide of happy people in a happy land, it is essential to spare no effort to discover and admit the reasons for suicide and to provide concrete factual evidence. The second part of these hearings is devoted directly to the crimes of the accused: why did he fail to notice in time the suicidal intention of his father, brother, daughter, neighbor, acquaintance, or compatriot, and why did he fail to prevent this Antiist act? At these trials there are often very moving scenes: unforgettable proofs of people's insight, psychological penetration, and accurate premonitions. From the point of view of Freedom, it is most important to train and develop the imagination, which becomes both the confirmation and the defense of Freedom in our life. It is particularly valuable that the untrammelled visionary quality of this imagination cannot easily be inherited or stolen; for every suicide has his own unique method of behaving and concealing his intentions and the means of their achievement.

Psychological trials can also be associated with those just mentioned as regards beauty and interest. These are trials where children give evidence against parents, parents against children, sisters against brothers, husbands against wives, wives against husbands, brother against brother, and so on. In trials of this kind, the duties of the spectators are usually performed by writers—in my opinion with indifferent success. In fact, the practical aim of such trials is to enable writers to study the general application of psychology. They are mainly quiet hearings, and the public, that is, the writers, sit with their notebooks on their knees and write down every word, without raising their heads. Only at the end, when the members of the court and the criminals have left the room, belated or purely intellectual applause can be heard.

Recently, psychological trials have been enriched by the acquisition of new subject matter—criminals of love and friendship. It would seem that love and friendship represent basic Satanoid methods; it would also appear that even free and happy people can never have enough of love and friendship, and our enemies know this very well. And so doubts have arisen as to whether we should renounce love for the sake of happiness and friendship for the sake of Freedom. Most people are prepared to do this, the more readily since a harmless method of loving is available; we can love babies, children who can't yet speak, and incurable invalids. It is also permissible to love parents and persons close to us in general when they are at the point of death. However, since we can never be completely sure that the dying person is not a deeply concealed Antiist who is using his last hour of life to inflict a poisonous wound, we prefer to concentrate all our feelings of love on babies and small children. Never in the history of the world has so much love been lavished on children as in Kamonia. Babies and children are half-crazy with happiness. The birth rate is very high; every woman is either pushing a pram or pregnant. As for our natural inclination and tendency to friendship, we do not renounce it; only we transfer it to other objects; instead of making friends with people, we do so with animals, things, and machines. Cats and dogs, birds and fishes, wildlife and rabbits, mice, tortoises and snakes have acquired an enormous significance in our lives, which they enrich emotionally and spiritually. In them, and with them, we find the fulfillment of our whole integrated human personality. In the animal world man finally becomes a real and sincere bearer of love, friendship, and mutual understanding. The movement for taming and breeding animals has become nationwide and is leading to new and exciting economic expansion. Almost overnight the land has become covered with farms for the selection and care of animals; and shops for the purchase and exchange of animals have become as common as food-shops. Capital is being redirected to the production and distribution of the "true friends of man," as this propaganda describes animals. Special institutes have sprung up for particular kinds of animals, and they are beginning to specialize in particular breeds and varieties; and there is now a vast literature dealing with the taming, training, cross-breeding, and rearing of animals. The entire morning television program is devoted to the selection and care of animals and the buying or selling of them. The owners of farms for red and yellow snakes have become millionaires and national figures, and the Forum of the Creators of History has enrolled them for life as honorary Supremely Happy. The price of red and yellow snakes is fantastic; if they are more than a yard long, they are not much cheaper than a two-seater airplane or one of the smaller ubimobiles. In the general pattern of our economic life, the constant rise in the value of shares in enterprises for the production of Super-Mice is outstanding. For His propaganda has no difficulty in convincing people that of all animals, mice can satisfy our human need for the expression of tenderness and loving-kindness with the minimum expenditure of money, time, and space. Mice are the cheapest friends, we hear, whenever we switch on the radio or the television. Mice keep us company, smiling at us from tunnel walls and hoardings, when we travel along any motorway in Kamonia. Our houses and gardens are full of all sorts of animals. We are always doing something with them—washing them, stroking them, playing with them. Our love and devotion to animals were quickly reflected in the rapid fall in the number of marriages and in the increased incidence of divorce; and also in the fall in the birth rate and the volume of tourist traffic.

But, as a result, our Happiness Balances are in a more favorable state than ever before.

Our love for animals has been accompanied by a passion for things, objects, or machines of all kinds. Despite a massive propaganda campaign in trade and industry, backed by scientists, and in particular by psychologists, to try and convince us that material objects are really the best and most devoted friends, and despite the seductive advertisements of flower-shops and market gardens for plants which show as Friends who are alive and beautiful, yet dumb and motionless, the position and importance of animals in Kamonia remains as basic as ever.

But even so, in spite of this general re-direction of our natural feelings of tenderness, our need to love and be loved, the number of offenses in connection with passionate love and romantic friendship continually increases. The more we fear love and friendship, the more criminals and Antiists there are. It is generally agreed that love is the internal destructive force for our happiness. I have therefore decided not to marry, since all the girls that attract me show such strong and passionate feelings of love that I cannot but doubt the purity of their incitement and intentions. Some of them, whose feelings were most extreme and who clearly wished to destroy my peace and happiness, I reported as "agent provocateurs" or future Antiists, and the court punished them accordingly. Attacks of romantic friendship have come to light even among the Protectors, the Happiest Citizens, the spectators at court, the Judges and other equally happy people. Every morning, in front of the relevant institutions, you can see long queues of people who have come to report provocative acts of love and friendship; and the queues are even longer after working hours. These crimes create new problems. The existing courts and Defensories are already being used beyond their capacity, and temporary Defensories and judicial premises have been set up in all our larger institutions.

From the scientific point of view, the most valuable trials are those connected with children on the verge of puberty and other potential Antiist material. The exciting and far-reaching nature of these trials lies in the choice of potential and future Antiist material. Here everything depends on the power of human foresight; unfortunately this is a very rare, indeed exceptional gift. Good will, the accustomed Freedom and current Happiness achieve relatively little in the aspect of the struggle for Total Victory. We are all convinced that the greatest scientific and artistic problem of our Freedom is to discover and disarm our potential future enemies.

The general spread of Antiism gives rise to all sorts of dissonant ideas in the minds of the free. Some people believe that Antiism is a pathological phenomenon, and that it should be regarded like any other illness and treated in the appropriate way. The Forum of the Creators of History has reacted promptly and decisively to this attitude, which it regards as naïve, stupid, and in the last resort, a form of sabotage.

Antiism is not a virus, as the Forum of the Creators of History tells us, from which we could defend ourselves by permanent immunization; it is in itself a sure sign that we are free and happy. Without Antiism it would be difficult for us to know how happy we are, and to continue the struggle for Total Victory and the Perfect Future. In addition, Antiism provides us with the objective conditions for the fulfillment of our free, many-sided, and creative personality, and confirms the absolute superiority of our Kamonian way of life over the wretched existence of the Satanoids. Hence Antiism brings us the excitement, surprise, and joys of victory—the most lasting joys there are.

The people of Kamonia have greeted these new directives with enormous enthusiasm, and the Palace of the Forums has been flooded with telegrams and messages of devotion, while the adherents of the idea that Antiism is a pathological phenomenon are being denounced and condemned.

All this has added fuel to the flames of the struggle against Satanoid influence from abroad. The frontiers of Kamonia are completely closed. As we have an abundance of everything we need, trade with foreign countries is unnecessary; it is true we lack certain spices and diamonds, but our Kamonian technology has succeeded in producing these artificially, and of a higher quality than the natural products, so that we have freed ourselves from the last trace of dependence on the Satanoid world. The Satanoids can still exercise their hostile influence only by way of our rivers, even though we have not bathed in rivers flowing from foreign countries for a long time now, nor eaten fish from them, nor even used their water for industrial purposes or irrigation. In accordance with their "Catonic Strategy," our General Staff has asked the Forum of the Creators of History to construct special filters at the frontiers to purify every drop of water coming from the Satanoid world, and special budgetary funds have been set aside for this purpose. In addition to this inspired measure, His Secret Order to the Space Academy to prevent winds from coming to our country from abroad—an order which has somehow trickled through the public, probably as a result of the free enthusiasm of the scientists—has further confirmed in us our feeling of unlimited power and invincibility. To this conviction has also contributed His Pronouncement concerning Antiism, that the view expressed by the Forum of the Creators of History that "the joys of victory are those that last longest" is the work of provocateurs and perfidious saboteurs; for this reason all those Creators of History who believed this and spoke in this way have been put on trial and shot. We are infinitely grateful to Him for convincing us that Antiism cannot bring joy in any shape or form, and so we have undertaken a final reckoning with all those who thought otherwise.

In addition to the conspiracies which are revealed nearly every month in the Forum of the Creators of the Future, the General Staff, the Academics, and Kamonia's other highest institutions, the wave of unmaskings of concealed Antiists has also affected the Protectory, its investigators, courts, and other judicial, state, and freedom organs. Because of the nature of the crime these trials last a long time and enable us to give full play to our temperament. At these trials we can harangue, shout, and swear to our hearts' content; we can even lynch the accused. These Antiists and conspirators from the highest places, the freest and the happiest, those whom we loved and trusted most after Him, convince us that there is no limit to human naïveté—otherwise there would have been an end of wickedness, unhappiness, and slavery. He has also taught us that the roots of Antiism are to be found in the remote past. We must uncover tham as well.

And so we are beset by a feeling of sacred duty as we are setting out in search of errors and criminals among our dead and distant ancestors. We study the past, biographies, chronicles, literature—bring to light documents concerning the ideas and nature of our ancestors, and we begin to try and condemn them. All our schools are being turned into courtrooms. The sentences bring us peace and alleviation. Nearly ninety per cent of our well-known ancestors against whom accusations have been leveled have been declared guilty and condemned to perpetual contempt and oblivion.

The Administration and members of the Bureau of Analysts, who have strikingly increased in numbers in recent years, have been shown in their pronouncements under the slogan "truth is a number" that there has been an increase in the number of malcontents among traditional intellectuals, especially philosophers, historians, and poets. This gives confirmation to lengthy human experience: knowledge is not to be found in books and cannot be learned with the mind; true knowledge is found in everyday life and is achieved by the work of hands and body. Nationwide anger against the intellectuals, the Forum of the Creators of the Future, is becoming more and more inflamed.

A new and, it is generally thought, protectionist policy is trying to shift the weight of responsibility in the task of uncovering concealed Antiists in the family circle; we all watch each other conscientiously, seizing upon every word and intonation, every movement, every crumb of thought, all shades and changes of mood. Before and after dinner, we discuss our observations and suspicions and accuse each other, giving evidence and judgment and proclaiming each other criminals even before the offenders are brought before the protectors and the court. In fact, our homes have become courts—our dining-rooms, beds, bathrooms, kitchens, and the rest—and courts of high judicial instance at that. Some authorities assert that these family courts outdo the customary classical ones as regards the severity of the accusations, the plausibility of the evidence, and the harshness of the punishments. Certain problems of a formal nature arise in families consisting of only a husband and wife, or a mother and daughter, since their sentences do not fulfill the required legal conditions; the accused have no one to defend them. Some complementary procedure is therefore necessary. The weekly illustrated magazines are full of descriptions of lyrical and romantic judgments between old married couples, who only after fifty years of bed and board together have discovered that their partner is an Antiist, without Happiness and Freedom. The accounts of the unmasking of the future Antiists among young married couples are no less moving and interesting. Many exploits in the defense of Freedom are carried out even during the honeymoon.

The customary and natural manner of expression for a free and happy man is to speak everything out aloud, even the most intimate and shameful matters; no one whispers any more, even while embracing, or in bed, or in the performance of their marital duties: so that no suspicions may be aroused, everything must be audible; even children must hear the truth, even the neighbors know what we feel and think. This free behavior has had a radical effect on all customs, habits, and relationships. For instance, a few people want to live alone in a house, a flat, or a room: people offer flats to live in, invite guests, and visit each other constantly; they entreat, give money or bribes, and go to all lengths in order to live in the largest possible units, and never to sleep with only one other person. These needs and desires are revolutionizing the architecture and the interior arrangements of houses and flats; nearly all the traditional forms of furniture and fittings are being abandoned; doors and windows are being removed, and only put in position if the weather is very bad, and then only by timid persons or those in poor health. Houses and flats of transparent material fetch a high price. Whole streets and estates are being built of completely transparent houses with total audiovisual sets. Whereas at first the Protectors used to install total audiovisualizers secretly in houses and public places, we do this openly and freely and voluntarily. The installation of total audiovisualizers is regarded as evidence of our high standard of living, and we are happy that our citizens of Kamonia are the only people in the world who can freely install total audiovisual sets which are linked up with the Kamonian Central Information Service.

The Forum of the Creators of the Future is bringing in a Five Year Plan for Total Audiovisualization, according to which it is proposed to install audiovisualators not only in all public places and highways, but in all picnic areas, woods, river banks, lake shores, and at the seaside. In addition to this State Plan, there is a powerful private industry for producing devices to secure intimate information. The National Corporation for the exchange of personal facts and the Verification Bureau for them have become, as it were overnight, large concerns with big profits. Psychology, particularly psychosynthesis, is not the leading science in Kamonia. But Industry and Commerce, Science, and the Skilled Trades are closely followed in this respect by the Arts, particularly by the Seven-Dimensional Film and Somnovision, which by their thematic structure are primarily and universally informative.

For we cannot be free and happy if we are unaware of what the people around us are thinking about us, and, if we have no knowledge of the thought and feelings of the people with whom we live and work, and whom we meet and see regularly. To be really free, we must know everything, without exception: dreams, food-menus, sex and family relationships, quarrels, intentions, wishes, passions, jokes. For this purpose we have to equip ourselves with the appropriate technical devices. We buy, sell, and exchange information and facts. Curiosity about intimate secrets, and their revelation and documentation, is becoming a universal and national passion, which has made many Kamonian citizens millionaires and extremely powerful figures; in fact there is no longer any doubt that the richest and most powerful people in Kamonia are those who know most about others. Also working total audiovisualizers has become our favorite pastime. They have reached such a stage of technical perfection that by merely twiddling a knob we can see and hear what is being said, whispered, and done in any house in any part of Kamonia, together with the corresponding colors and smells. We usually spend our evenings in this way, and this has resulted in an abrupt decline of interest in the theatre, cinema, television, somnovision, and concerts. The foundation of a Somnocenter where, one by one in order of our arrival, we relate and discuss our dreams before a large public, has brought us new joys, and increased our Freedom even more. Attempts are being made to meet the need, which is growing exceptionally rapidly, for such centers, by organizing circles for the narration and discussion of dreams in groups of houses and blocks of flats. But nobody is satisfied by these improvised arrangements, above all because of the inadequacies of the audience, so the Forum of the Creators of the Future is being asked to make increased investment in the building of somnocenters.

The unmasking this year of the sixth conspiracy against Him in the Forum of the Creators of History and of the Future, in the General Staff, and in His personal bodyguard of the Protectory, and the third conspiracy running of the Silent Left has convinced us that the Satanoids are stubbornly resolved to destroy our Happiness. But He has made public his Salvationary Thesis and his Prophetic Message to us: it is widely known what conditions are like in the Satanoid world. No less well known are the conditions in those countries where the people believe that they have the best of everything. To recapitulate:

FIRSTLY, THE SINGLE STATE

Its people are only numbers. They have a number for both surname and Christian name, because they have no individual characteristics. They all wear the same uniform. Love is forbidden. Sex is rationed and distributed by coupons. The use of coffee, alcohol, and tobacco is forbidden. The people are deprived of all emotional life. Imagination is forbidden, and people are treated for it like any other disease. Life for the Benefactor is instilled by mechanical means. All aspects of life are under police control.

This order of things requires no comment.

SECONDLY, OCEANIA

Although the standard of living is relatively high, poverty and inequality are the rule. A man need not be poor and unhappy, but he is because this is Big Brother's wish. And Big Brother has a compulsive need to do only evil. In this society sadism and efficiently organized tyranny prevail.

Again, no comment on this order of things is required.

THIRDLY, THE WORLD STATE

Technology has annihilated man. He no longer knows anything of mother-love, family life, morals, or natural emotions. No one knows what spontaneous passion is. People are produced in laboratories, according to a well-ordained plan. They are all alike, and everyone belongs to everyone else. Their only games are with machines. Joy and excitement are bought at the drug store.

Again, no comment is required on this technocratic order of things.

What do the best among the Satanoids believe? They believe that Happiness and Freedom are irreconcilable. Their naïve folly is to be pitied.

What do we believe? We believe that Freedom and Happiness are indivisible. Only Antiism is irreconcilable with them.

What do the best among the Satanoids assert? They hold that power is an end in itself and that power only exists for the sake of one man's power over another. This is clearly an abomination.

What do we hold? We say that power is neither a means nor an end.

What is the general conclusion? It is clearly self-evident.

We were so delighted by the depth of His thought and the elegance of His style that we decorated all our buildings—factories, churches, offices, and block of flats—with the slogans: This order of things requires no comment. Their naïve folly is pitiful. This is clearly an abomination. It is clearly self-evident. These last words of wisdom have particularly impressed us, and we have begun to greet each other with them. They have also furnished both the title and the subject matter for many poems and doctoral theses; and we have been promised an opera and a number of cantatas based on the same words—"it is clearly self-evident"—in the near future.

In his Prophetic Work concerning Us, He has condensed into two sentences the content of a multitude of books and said everything that any man needs to know, so as never to err in any way.

Everybody can be Happy, but not everybody can be an Antiist. Anyone who is not Happy is an Antiist.

All of us have studied these supreme truths, which form the hub of our scientific, intellectual, and artistic life, and the basis of a new industry of ideas and morals. This spirit inspires scenarios and dramas, the production of films and plays, and the composition of symphonies and songs.

A New Era has begun—the universal liquidation of the unhappy. All those who for any reason are not happy, or whose Happiness is in any way dubious, are denounced to the Protector and brought to trial and judgment. Accusations of crimes of the following type are particularly numerous: he didn't laugh at my joke; he wept too much at his child's funeral; he breathes heavily or yawns or moans in his sleep.

Since the existing capacity of the courts is inadequate to deal with new offenders and Antiists, the Forum of the Creators of History has announced its decision that a number of trains, tramcars, and buses should be turned into courts. The advantage of these new types of courts is that they are mobile and can be concentrated in the places where the number of criminals is greatest. Trains have a special technical advantage; they can stand in sidings in the stations, and each coach can be labeled with a special category of crime, lapse, or error, while the individual compartments, which make very intimate courts, are used when specifically required for the narrower fields of responsibility in any offense. Sometimes these courts—as soon as they contain the requisite number of people and carry the optimum weight—are used to transport Antiists to their prescribed destination.

While the Satanoid world, we are convinced, is in the grip of universal poverty, hunger, and epidemic disease, and is torn by strikes, revolts and terror, we in Kamonia live in plenty. We have everything we need. The official organ of the Forum of the Creators of History, the radio, the television, and the psychovision repeat the Forum's proclamation every morning:

At all times and in all places, say what you want. Ask that all your wishes should be fulfilled. Invent things that will make you even happier. Buy more than you have money for. Buy everything that is for sale. Spend more than you earn. Whatever and however much you have, want to have something else, and more. Keep on buying everything and spending continuously.

In the Forum's Reform Associations and Observations, from waking to the beginning of work, when a considerable number of people are morose, ill-inclined, and even anxious, Two Optimistic

Instructions are given: Think what you will buy today; and Record both what is ugly and what is beautiful.

And we buy, spend, or record. We don't know what to do with all the food and clothes, furniture and machines, cars and gadgets; but we buy them, because every day something new and different appears; because: other people are buying things, everybody is buying things; because: if we are not always spending money, we are not happy. Today we are eating purple bread, because it has been advertised as the bread eaten by happy people; we drink "helio-juice" because it is said to strengthen sexual powers and to maintain them all one's life; we use "Chloromol" soap because it is said to arouse lyrical dreams. And when the next day we hear that red bread is the bread eaten by outstanding people, we buy it; that the cosmic boxing champion's favorite drink is "Python Blood," we buy that, too; that "Sturgeon's Eye" soap was used by Cleopatra and St. Augustine, we buy that soap. In fact, the general belief is that anyone who does not spend much or buys little, who does not buy a new psychovision, a new ubimobile, new gadgets, new machines, and methods of amusement, anyone who thinks he has enough money, is not a true Kamonian. Such people are universally regarded with suspicion, and publicly branded, derided, boycotted, and condemned.

As well as buying things, at the same time, we follow the Forum's Second Optimistic Instruction and uninterruptedly record all that we see and hear. Already sixty-eight per cent of our average life is recorded; according to the plan of the Forum of the Creator of the Future, in the course of the next ten years, there will be a publicly and privately produced audiovisual record of ninety-six per cent of human life so that, for all practical purposes, nothing will be left unrecorded. In addition to giving us amusement while we look at photographs and films of scenes and places we have seen, and listening to the noise of the streets, conversations in shops, concerts, masses, private conversations, jokes and laughter, our films and tapes will be at the disposal of analysts, psychosyn-thetists, and the Protectory for them to study and establish the corresponding facts and conclusions. The results are incalculable. In all probability, traditional witnesses, judges, and courts will be abolished. On the basis of photographs, films, and material provided by total audiovisualators, everything will be scientifically analyzed in the laboratories, all our needs, habits, and wishes will become known, and it will be possible to establish exactly our convictions, moods, and behavior to know where we have been and with whom we did and said. In short, there will be an accurate factual and permanent record of whom we are and what we are. And that will have, and indeed already has, inestimably progressive results, as well as influencing our economy, arts, science, law, and religion.

Translated by Muriel Heppel

DUŠAN RADOVIĆ

(b. 1922)

Radović was born in Niš. He is a poet and satirist. His literary opus, although not voluminous, has made an important impression on the development of Yugoslav contemporary poetry and satire. His work became known, through television, to a huge audience. Radović is one of the pioneering writers who cast off the traditional methods of writing of poetry and built a modern way of writing, concise and simple in the extreme. His literary works as a whole speak about the child: the child is appreciated and respected as a personality; imagination and play are the primary elements of the world and life in general; mystery, curiosity, and strangeness, and, particularly, "playful excitement of language, ennobled didacticism, fantasy, and gay seriousness" characterize his writings.

His books include *Respected Children* (1954), *Funny Words* (1962), stories entitled *I'm Telling You a Story* (1963), and a play *Captain John Peoplefolks* (1965).

In his satirical writings, Radović is original and modern: his witty playing on words reaches nonsense; his style is free from restraints and rules. This makes his satirical works some of the most popular in Yugoslavia at the present time.

Monkeys

ONCE UPON A TIME, monkeys did not have any tails.

They had tails, but they were not actually tails, but real umbrellas. They were colorful and nice looking and they opened and closed.

When it was raining, all the animals got wet; only the monkeys opened up their umbrellas and huddled under them.

When the sun was beaming, the monkeys were dozing in the shade, under the shelter of their umbrellas.

They enjoyed themselves.

Each monkey had a little umbrella.

But, since monkeys live in the forests and since there are numerous trees in the forests and since the trees are composed of branches and since the monkeys constantly jump from one branch to the next, the umbrellas kept tearing apart. They were never beautiful and new.

They were torn apart again and again, until they tore apart completely.

Other umbrellas did not want to grow, so that only the handle remained.

The monkeys, of course, cried. They were depressed.

At the beginning, they did not know what to do with the handles of the umbrellas. But suddenly it occurred to them.

They hitched themselves onto a branch with these handles and hung upside down.

This was funny to them, and they laughed.

This is how it used to be.

This is how it is.

This is how it is always going to be.

Translated by Branko Mikasinovich

A Little Finger

THE LITTLE KIDS were bored.

Against the boredom of kids, we invented toys.

One kind of toy is scissors. With the scissors, one can cut: books, dresses, and fingers.

The second toy is a hammer. With the hammer one can bang: nails, walls, and also fingers.

The third toy is matches. With matches one can burn: dresses, covers, and again fingers.

Children are small, but their fingers are the smallest.

Once upon a time, there was a finger and his name was Djura. He had a lot of brothers. A lot—for sure more than six.

Once, the brothers took Djura to the desk drawer. Djura left last, and he nipped his nail.

The second time, they took him into the oven to see if it were hot. So Djura got burned.

The third time they played with a needle. All of them avoided it, but Djura pricked himself.

Djura, Djura, you are not the worst finger!

He is.

When one needs to pick the nose—let Djura do it.

When one has to feel how cold the water is—push Djura to do it.

But, when one has to dip the fingers into the jelly, then it is done by some other fingers, but not Djura.

Djura got to the point where he had had enough. It was enough. He won't tolerate it any more.

All kids have this Djura; that is, the fifth finger, the smallest.

He is not for work, but for joy.

He started playing piano. He is joking, and he is spoiled. Let him be like that—he is small.

Translated by Branko Mikasinovich

VASA POPOVIĆ

(b. 1923)

Vasa Popović was born in Jazak, Serbia. He works as a newspaper man in Belgrade and has been a contributor to numerous papers and magazines throughout Yugoslavia. Popović is a master of short satirical and humorous stories.

Some of his better known works are: *People Like One Another* (1954), *Philip on a Horse* (1960), and *I Do Not Want to Get a Haircut* (1964).

Popović satires have had a strong social impact and political significance. "The Fenced Sea" is a story which provoked a fierce reaction against exclusive and private resort areas which were situated in the best regions of the Adriatic coast, thus forcing the rest of the citizens to be limited to less attractive places. The story had such an impact that it succeeded, in many instances, against private monopolization of the sea. Consequently, Popović, as a satirist, had performed the role of a "social reformer." Though "satirical" is an inadequate term for these multilayered creations, they can be called "documentary" sketches with awakening, ironic qualities.

The Fenced Sea

I ONCE READ SOMEWHERE, or I heard it and remembered it, that no man can change the world, and that every man changes from evil to good or from good to evil, in both ways throughout his life, and then dies. I read it a long time ago and remember it well, so that even today it happens that I often repeat these words. I repeat them subconsciously and absent-mindedly, without trying to understand them, but I repeat them simply and automatically till exhaustion. Every man is good in an evil society. I mean every man; I even include myself.

It occurred to me today here in Hvar. While it was raining, I was walking on the beach, and I said to myself, "Wait, wait, brother! What does it mean 'Every man is good in an evil society.' Are you a good person? How good are you?"

"I am as good as dust. How can dust be good?"

"There is no dust in Hvar." The shore is asphalted; the path is straight; it is a beautiful path for walking. The path has been asphalted even through the forest and the rain does not bother me. I smell the flowers and watch the birds. There are some strange birds, and I forget to ask the natives what they are called. There are small birds with reddish chests who became fat and resemble jumping beauties; they got fat from eating the caterpillars off the branches of the pine trees.

"Are these birds good? They are small. Beautiful! And, surely, they are good. And caterpillars, they, therefore, are not good. They are not, although they are interesting. The caterpillars are not good, but the birds are good.

I am strolling through the forest self-content, with thoughts that are not really thoughts (but they are pleasant and nice), and I feel nice here in Hvar. When I meet a dog, I pet it, and when the same dog wants to befriend me, but also wants to chase every cat, I chase it away. I chased away a cat, too, throwing small stones at it. It was a white and black cat; it walked gracefully, and I patted her shiny fur when I saw her the first time. She got away from my hands and caught a small bird. Afterwards, I pursued that cat every day.

She was impudent; she was constantly after small birds.

A good man in an evil world; he would want to make order and good behavior between the birds and the caterpillars and between the cats and the dogs. He is crazy—a good man in an evil world. But, perhaps the world is good and the man evil—nothing is for certain.

Enough of this nonsense; although, I admit, this nonsense is a beautiful recreation of my everyday existence.

Hvar's everyday existence is recuperation. Even walks are like a tonic.

She was impudent; she was constantly after small birds.

A good man in an evil world; he would want to make order and good behavior between the birds and the caterpillars and between the cats and the dogs. He is crazy—a good man in an evil world. But, perhaps the world is good, and the man, evil—nothing is for certain.

Enough of this nonsense; although, I admit, this nonsense is a beautiful recreation of my everyday existence.

Hvar's everyday existence is recuperation. Even walks are like a tonic.

But, it is good to plan our everyday existence on Hvar nicely and logically. I did not do it successfully; I stroll through the forest; the forest makes me mad because of the caterpillars and cats. Then I go to a tavern and stay there. That is bad. Through the tavern's windows I saw a well-known professor, strolling deliberately. Actually, he does not stroll; he paces swiftly with even steps; but then he was no longer in my sight. After ten minutes he returns, and then again repeats the same thing. He goes away and returns. He would walk for two entire hours until noon. When he appeared in the afternoon, I started following him. I am also strolling deliberately.

But I don't know how to pace evenly, not even when strolling; every moment I would look around. I don't know how to look in front of myself—in my steps—to relax my legs, to exercise them for strolling and for escaping. I walk for a while and stop. I see a bee; where does it fly in this rain? From flower to flower flies the little bee. What news! I could care less for such news! How much is honey? Are bees rewarded according to how much they produce? They work because they adore it. They are symbols of work, hard work; that is why man raises bees, because they produce honey. I do not like honey, so I do not like bees. I prefer grasshoppers; but grasshoppers do not "creek" when it is raining; I hate rain.

I started following the well-known professor, but he had already returned. Well, that means his path for strolling is short. I will then continue to the end of his path.

I am walking swiftly to exercise my legs, to rest my soul of everyday existence. A sudden wave hits the shore and my hat, and I am proud of my hat. Since a hat costs seven thousand dinars today (are rabbits selling their fur at such high prices?). Since my hat wrinkles an awful lot, it is not made from rabbit's fur. Our merchants cheated me. I feel like smashing my hat in our Adriatic Sea; let the waves take it to Italy. There such a hat would cost only two thousand liras. Those Italians, as if they are better than we are!

The professor returned in his swift walk and bypassed me. I am trying to follow at the same tempo. I am passing him. I am not going to return with him. I will walk around the whole island.

I have already been walking swiftly for three minutes. I pass a curve, and then I have to stop. The professor also stopped. Some kind of fence barred my path.

Not too loudly, I ask myself, "Where does this fence come from?"

The professor was staring for a moment over the fence and started walking back swiftly.

"Who fenced the sea? What is this behind this fence?" I thought to myself. But, I see it myself; behind the fence is a blue sea; the bluest in Hvar; the bluest beach in Hvar.

"What is this fence?" I asked a nearby fisherman.

"This is a resort place for the officials of the Croatian parliament," says the man. "They made a fence around the building and they also fenced the beach."

The Fenced Sea. I cannot go any further here. There is a fence. I cannot go to the left—there is water. I wanted to walk further, but can't.

Why have they fenced the sea? Why do they need the fence? As if somebody likes to be behind a fence. Nonsense. Nobody likes that. Actually, and in principle, nobody likes to be fenced by some fence. Nobody likes a fence erected before his nose.

I wanted to walk further, along the whole beach of Hvar, but I could not. It was ridiculous and tragic.

I felt sorry, so sorry that I wanted to see the building which they fenced. The building is not handsome; it is big, but not handsome. I saw that it was not handsome. I do not like it. The architect who built it should forgive me for this. He did not succeed. I think that he had no taste.

On the other hand, respect is due the architect who built a small stone house, seven meters by five, not too far away from here. That is a nice house; good style and good size.

I wanted, I really wanted to take off my hat, to greet that little house. But I did not greet it. My hat was wet, very wet, so I thought, "Why should I remove my wet hat? What is there to greet when they fenced the sea? And, then, nobody is in the little stone house. Neither is there anyone in the big house now. Who is there to greet and for what? Let my wet hat stay on my head as long as it will."

Translated by Branko Mikasinovich

ALEKSANDAR POPOVIĆ
(b. 1928)

Popović was born in Ub, Serbia. He started writing in 1950 and was the first author to introduce light humor and Serbian slang into his works. He is considered to be the founder of contemporary Yugoslav satirical plays.

Popović's works marked a new direction in satirical writings. He introduced personages from everyday life, people from the streets who dealt with ordinary matters. His satire is framed within his plays, similar to burlesque and vaudeville, complete with low comedy and vulgarity. While Popović's satire is based on the idea that one learns easily when one laughs, Popović's *Hats Off!* (1967) is a protest against mechanization, bureaucracy, and automated life and sex.

The popularity and effectiveness of *Hats Off!* lies in Popović's ability to use current and proverbial expressions. Popović rapidly alters his themes and subject matter, with little regard for the form or content, stressing only the values of the humorous and the satirical.

HATS OFF!

Theatrical Vespers in Two Acts
(Waste and Halter)

CHARACTERS

Macabre—All-Power

Two-Ton Honey

Adagio—The Court-Bawdy-O

Flirty-Gertie

Eugene—Man of Mystery

Artie Fartie

Seven Maids Who've Never Been Laid

There's more guessing than messing, but it all goes up in smoke anyway.

ACT I: WASTE

(On by Day—Off by Night)

*(*MACABRE'S *Court. Nightmarish confusion.)*

THE SEVEN MAIDS *(Singing and dancing)*:

> On my coat a hundred patches,
> Every debtor has his snatches!...
> People think that it's a joke,
> That I'm absolutely broke,
> But I have one hundred grand—
> Grains!—pure Adriatic sand!

MACABRE: Wham!...*(The confusion abates.* THE SEVEN MAIDS, MACABRE, *and* HONEY *exit.)*

ADAGIO *(Stays behind with* GERTIE *to clean up the mess.* ARTIE *droops on the throne):* I feel as if I'd been raped by the Seventh Fleet.

GERTIE: That's what I call wishful thinking!

ADAGIO: We work our fingers to the bone, and they plunder us in our own house!

GERTIE: The floor boards creak under their feet!

ADAGIO: And the pillow reeks under their cheeks, like rotten fish in a porcelain dish!

MACABRE: Give me your hand!

GERTIE: Yeah!...as they say "Right makes might!" But why waste breath. Just let everything follow its own fine course, right down to rack and ruin!

ADAGIO: Come on, let's have it, bandmaster! Toast each in turn! Music!... *(Music.)* First toast to the host! *(Music.)*

GERTIE: And his wife—but not for life! *(Music.)*

ADAGIO: To the brass on their ass, and the cops in heat on their beat. *(Music.)*

GERTIE: And the tinker, tailor, soldier, sailor! *(Music.)*

ADAGIO: Rich man, poor man, beggar man, thief! *(Flourish of trumpets, pompous gallop.)*

MACABRE *(Enters doing the gallop):* Come on now, let old Dad take you for a little walk through history!

GERTIE: That's Macabre, the head-codger around here!

MACABRE: Give me some skin!

ADAGIO: And get your knuckles rapped!

MACABRE: Adagio!

ADAGIO *(Jumps forward and dances about* MACABRE*):* At your service, Right Reverend!

MACABRE: You sinner, you! *(Exits.)*

ADAGIO *(Jumps off after* MACABRE*):* My only sin is that I'm forever longing for your whip!

HONEY *(She appears at the same moment and looks back at* ADAGIO*):* What are you prancing about for, Adagio?

GERTIE: That's Two-Ton Honey—Macabre's second wife in order of running, but now she's the apple of his eye. They call her Cunty-Honey as a pet name.

MACABRE *(Enters,* ADAGIO *saunters after him):* Cunty-Honey, I can't stand to look at him doing a jig like that!

HONEY: Like a cat on a hot tin roof...phooey! *(Exits.)*

MACABRE *(To* ADAGIO*):* You heard her, first go pee on a tree, and then come!

ADAGIO: I won't! I like to struggle with nature.

GERTIE: In the daylight, he can face anything; I should know! For me he's a real man! But as soon as it gets dark, he wets himself. He goes all to pieces from one caress...and I'm like his wife, humph! *(Exits.)*

MACABRE *(To* ADAGIO*):* You're laying yourself wide open, Adagio. I hope you can hold out!

ADAGIO: Even if I have to help myself a little with my hand, I won't let you down!

MACABRE: And now go ask if he wants anything.

ADAGIO: I know Artie's answer without even asking him: he loves silk pants better than a silk gown.

MACABRE: Keep knowledge like that to yourself. You'll need it, and ask him like I told you to! *(*GERTIE *enters.* ARTIE *comes on the ramp accompanied by a gallop.)*

GERTIE: That's somebody called Artie. Actually he's Macabre's son by wife number one, but he's in the doghouse here now!

ADAGIO *(Bows before* ARTIE*):* Is there anything the young bull desires?

ARTIE: You must help me exterminate them all! *(Exits. ADAGIO dances out after him.)*

MACABRE *(Enters with GERTIE):* You must persuade him to run off with you!

GERTIE: Who'll inflame your old blood if I go?

MACABRE: I'll watch dirty movies! In the meantime I'll disown him by surprise. He won't be my son any more! *(Exits, followed by GERTIE.)*

HONEY *(Enters with ARTIE):* Macabre is on his last legs...he'd like to, but he can't....

ARTIE: It doesn't matter, I can do it for the both of us. You don't lose a thing!

HONEY: I know, but then he strains at it all day long...and he has monkey glands implanted, and he pushes, gets all red in the face, the veins in his neck almost burst...and he pants like a dog in the sun....

ARTIE: Well, if all bugs were to shit honey, what would happen to the bumble-bee?

HONEY: That's it! We just have to catch him spent on the mattress with that bitch. Then it's a bullet in the forehead for her, and a muzzle and a leash for him! *(Exits, followed by ARTIE.)*

MACABRE *(Enters with ADAGIO):* You're young, and she's an old woman!

ADAGIO: You don't get it for nothing—even from an old bag!

MACABRE: You're wrong; an old woman takes what she can get. She won't turn anything down. That'll be my corpus delicti, to get rid of her! *(Exits, followed by ADAGIO.)*

HONEY *(Enters with GERTIE):* What about making love with both the father and the son!

GERTIE: And the Holy Ghost! He left me heavy once, and nobody ever believed me!

HONEY: Don't worry: you've got sex coming out of your ears! They'll tear each other to pieces over you, like wild boars in heat! *(Exits, followed by GERTIE.)*

MACABRE *(Enters, followed by ARTIE):* You've got to help me liquidate these conspirators, Son!

ARTIE: Which ones?

MACABRE: Honey is thick with Gertie. And Adagio is worming

his way into her confidence! They're all in cahoots! They ought to be shot! *(Exits, followed by* Artie.*)*

HONEY *(Enters with* Adagio*):* Kill the bastards when they least expect it, and you'll have a place in my bed guaranteed!

ADAGIO: Don't think that I'm haggling, but I've had better offers.

Honey: Don't get excited: let me finish. . . . On top of that you'll get an apartment and a warm bed, all for free!

ADAGIO: What about my commission?

HONEY: Well, it all depends on the service rendered, what kind of showing you make. *(Exits, goes off, followed by* Adagio. *)*

ARTIE *(Enters, followed by* Gertie*):* Adagio is cheating on you, Gertie. . . . He could very well get you in big trouble. Better to kill him today than to kill someone else's crabs on you tomorrow! As for me, I'll bump off Honey—and then we can get to the elections with an easy mind!

GERTIE: Macabre is sure to be the top candidate anyway, and we know that the masses always blindly go for the first man. And then he'll be sitting pretty. . . . A lot of good that will do you. . . . And you, you'll stand on the sidelines, green with envy!

ARTIE: But if we just light a firecracker under his seat, that'll make things hot for him. The old man has one foot in the grave already. One more shove and he'll topple into the hole, and then we two are left to run the show. *(Exits, followed by* Gertie.*)*

HONEY *(Enters with* Macabre*):* Well, are you deaf and dumb?

EUGENE *(Peers out):* Mooooo!

MACABRE: Concentrations of motorized birds of prey have been observed around the borders. And the beast in me has been ominously gnashing its teeth for three days now. I must take a look into this. *(Exits.)*

EUGENE *(Peers out):* Mooooo! *(Charges* Honey, *she steps aside and he runs past.)* Mooooo!

HONEY: Let's see if it'll make him wiser if he knocks his head against the wall?

EUGENE *(Rushes at* Honey*)* Mooooo! *(She dodges him. He runs past and hits his head on the wall.)*

HONEY: That should calm him down now!

EUGENE *(Hops about):* Moooo!

HONEY: What a thick skull! *(Takes off her red skirt and remains in her panties.)* Maybe he'll chase a skirt on a stick? *(Puts her skirt on a stick and leads* EUGENE *through a Veronica with a Flourish of Brass.)*

EUGENE: Mooooo!... Mooooo!... *(In the end* HONEY *conquers him.)*

HONEY: Who are you?

EUGENE: A big ox. Mooooo!

HONEY: Just as I thought: a nobody. Raw potential! But I'll put you in the big time. Just let them get used to you, and then you'll weave spider webs around them after my pattern!

EUGENE: What do I get for it? What's in it for me?

HONEY: A higher standard of living.

EUGENE: I'll fight for my bacon and for my butter! I'll fight for my car and my TV set! I'll fight to the last gasp! *(*HONEY *exits and he obediently follows her.)* Mooooo!

MACABRE *(Enters):* The tourists have swarmed all over, and all they do is click-click with their cameras. They shoot at everything they see!

HONEY *(Enters):* Even the birth rate has gone out of control; everything is going down the drain; pretty soon we'll be eating one another!

MACABRE: Everybody's gotten into a uniform; you can't tell her from him anymore!

HONEY: The worst of all is that everyone has his heart set on your speedy end—I must tell you that, though I know it's not pleasant to hear.

MACABRE: Well, we'll have to see about that!

HONEY: All right, but don't forget afterwards, when spoils are shared out, who first warned you about what can happen.

MACABRE: I'll give everyone his measure.

HONEY: That's precisely what I'm saying, this is where you're wrong: you don't measure your friends with yardsticks across their backs! *(Exits.)*

MACABRE *(After her):* Would you, Cunty-Honey, be the only one to wish me well? I'm a bit suspicious about your unnatural interest in all this. *(Exits.)*

ADAGIO *(Enters with* GERTIE*):* My poor little Gertie, just look at it! Why here it's all for none and nobody for all! Who'll live through all this? *(Exits.)*

GERTIE: Me—that's who! Because, when it comes to a free-for-all, I'm all for free! Let there be music, and let the wine flow: come on...music! *(Music.)*

MACABRE *(Enters with* Artie, Honey, *and* Eugene*):* The old clock on the wall says it's time for bed!

EUGENE: Mooooo! *(Everyone undresses. Striptease.)*

MACABRE *(To* Artie, *who is already in his underpants):* You've already got your pants off?

ARTIE *(Embarrassed):* Well, someone asked me:

> "Artie, my boy,
> "Show me your toy.
> Don't be so coy!"

HONEY *(She and* Gertie *quickly gather up their things and cover themselves in embarrassment):* Is there no love without insult? *(Exits.)*

GERTIE: This is an insult! He offered me his life if I would be his wife! *(Exits.)*

ARTIE: I was pulling their leg, honest, Dad!

MACABRE: I believe you, my boy, but, nevertheless, I ask you: where's your honor? Where's your dignity?

ARTIE *(Gets dressed quickly):* It's all because of them! I could easily catch cold!

MACABRE: If she's as naked as a jaybird, your pants won't be in the way! Besides, you and I must still appear on the rostrum.

GERTIE *(Enters):* Where's the pail?

ADAGIO *(Enters, bringing the pail):* Have I got to be a chambermaid now? *(To* Honey.*)* Your grace has expressed the desire to ease herself before going to bed. *(*Honey *goes off,* Adagio *follows her with the pail.* Macabre *and* Artie *mount the two rostrums at either side of the stage.)*

MACABRE *(From the rostrum):* Why?... but why?... but why does man live?

ARTIE *(From the rostrum):* Why? Why? Why, so he can give!

MACABRE: But if he's to give and give, how will he get rich?

ARTIE: By walking on water and avoiding the ditch!

MACABRE: And the wind is strong! But in case, there's a wind blowin'?

MACABRE AND ARTIE *(Sing the end in a duet):* And there's nothing to throw in? No use rowin'—try floatin'! *(They slowly descend from the rostrums. Music.* GERTIE *enters quietly, bringing along* THE SEVEN MAIDS.*)*

GERTIE *(To* THE MAIDS*):* Come on now, girls, open up!

THE SEVEN MAIDS AND GERTIE *(Dance and sing like fairies around* MACABRE, *who acts as if it were all just a dream.* AR-TIE *slumps down on his throne):*

> None but the brave
> Deserves to rave.
> None but the slave
> Deserves to crave.
> Down at the altar
> One dons the halter,
> God help who falter!

> Fire, fire, we desire
> Love and life to acquire.
> Dance, dance, now's our chance!
> Breeze, breeze, will you please
> Give us wings to fly and tease!
> Dance, dance, now's our chance!

(They ply their charms on MACABRE.*)*

MACABRE: You're like will-o'-the-wisps; you don't excite me a bit!

GERTIE AND THE SEVEN MAIDS *(In a frenzy):*

> Earth, earth, for all it's worth
> Give us love to foster birth.
> Dance, dance, now's our chance!

MACABRE: You send chills down my spine! But so do snakes!

GERTIE AND THE SEVEN MAIDS *(Still more furiously):*

> Water, water, the earth's daughter,
> That old codger almost caught her!
> Dance, dance, now's our chance!

MACABRE *(Manages to escape from them and flees off stage):* I'll make you sorry—you'll see! *(*The Maids *become silent.)*

ARTIE *(Rouses himself on the throne):* Gertie!

GERTIE *(Rushes to him):* Just say the word and I'm yours, but be nice to me.

ARTIE: Listen to me, Gertie, and I won't beat you.

GERTIE: But, if you're a friend, don't try to get something for nothing.

ARTIE *(Sharply):* What are you hiding in your slip?

GERTIE: Two bunches of grapes.

ARTIE: And I'm a wine-press! Come on; let's go!

GERTIE: I don't feel like it!

ARTIE: You want new love, but won't give up the old one!

GERTIE: I can't give up what I've never had!

GERTIE AND THE SEVEN MAIDS *(They dance seductively, in order to overwhelm* Artie*):*

> Sun, sun, mighty sun!
> Pop your gun—have some fun!
> Dance, dance, now's our chance!

*(*Artie *acts as if it were all just a dream. He tries to catch* Gertie, *but she always eludes him.)*

ARTIE: Don't try to escape, my little witch! *(*The maids *settle down.)* Come here and let me kiss you!...Why are you running away?

GERTIE: Because it's not very far from here to there! From the lips to the hips!

ARTIE: You're very edgy this morning; I know who's to blame!

GERTIE: He hasn't made love to me for over a week!

GERTIE AND THE SEVEN MAIDS *(They dance seductively, in order to overwhelm* Artie*):*

> Lonely and forsaken,
> Lips that aren't taken!
> Lonely and forsaken,
> Lips that aren't taken!

*(*Artie *acts as if it were all in a dream, tries to catch* Gertie, *but without success. Then all at once he stops and "wakes up.")*

ARTIE: That's enough!!! *(THE MAIDS scatter.)*

GERTIE: What's the matter with you?

ARTIE: What's the matter with *you*? You dance, you sing, and in the cupboard there's not a thing! Like sparks: now you see them, now you don't.... And me, overcome with sorrow....

GERTIE: You should be, but it's all the same to me.

ARTIE: What's garbage today will burn green with life tomorrow!

MACABRE *(Suddenly appears on the rostrum):* But this green fire will wane! *(ARTIE quickly climbs up on the other rostrum.)* Just ashes and cinders will remain!

ARTIE: *(From the rostrum):* Autumn and frost will come!

MACABRE: And I won't be on this platform anymore.

MACABRE AND ARTIE *(Sing the end in a duet):* And I'll belong to the long, long past oblivion—oblivion.... *(ARTIE disappears from the rostrum, and MACABRE slowly descends to the stage. The MAIDS quietly leave the stage, and GERTIE comes forward to meet MACABRE.)*

GERTIE: Do you know what's good for marble, Macabre?

MACABRE: No, unless it's a good woman's warm bottom?

GERTIE: A good try, but off the mark! I'll tell you, but the one who does it should think of me when I'm no longer here.

MACABRE: Are you talking about your tombstone or mine?

GERTIE: About yours, Macabre! About yours! Just state in your will that your tombstone is to be rubbed with a linen rag and turpentine—and it'll shine like crystal! And, as for me, just let them say: "Gertie taught us that once a long time ago." *(ADAGIO runs across the stage.)* Why is that man flitting around like a madman again?

MACABRE *(ADAGIO runs across the stage again):* Adagio, is that you in the depths of nocturnal stillness?

GERTIE: Is he rushing about again because of the chamber pot?

ADAGIO *(Rushes to them):* Dan's been killed!... fishing in the river.... Someone must have shortened the fuse!

GERTIE *(Whispers to ADAGIO):* Not like that, for heaven's sake, sugar the pill!

MACABRE: Send a deputation and, in token of humility, let them wash dishes over the open grave!

ADAGIO: But in what connotation?

MACABRE: In the spirit of: my nose is clean.

ADAGIO: So he died of a natural accident!

MACABRE: And every delegate must wear a black band on his heel!

GERTIE *(Softly to* ADAGIO*):* Take it easy, man. Never mention horns in the home of a cuckold! *(Exits.)*

ADAGIO: And, as I was saying, a grenade went off in his hand. He didn't have time to throw it away in the river.

MACABRE: I smell sabotage, Gertie!

GERTIE *(Enters):* If my vote counts for anything, I say get the fool out of here! *(Exits.)*

MACABRE: But this must be done with style. Get the bastard out!

ADAGIO: Let's not be hasty! We might break the ceiling!

MACABRE: I won't deny myself anything. When I talk about tightening the belt, that only goes for other people.

ADAGIO: Well, put the thumb on your boys.

MACABRE: Sure, but how can I be happy if everyone around me is unhappy? They'll turn everything sour!

ADAGIO: All right...but we've got to get some idea. We'll need approximately about a hundred odd skewers. At least there's no shortage of poltroons. And with astronomical figures, one more or less won't make any difference!

MACABRE: Gertie! *(*GERTIE *enters.)* Have you pulled down the fence?

GERTIE: Fanny fell off the fence on a phallic fish!

MACABRE: Good thing it didn't fracture its fins! Come on, bring a glass for Adagio and a bottle of rot gut. Let's drink to the ratification and set our minds at ease. *(*ADAGIO *goes off.)*

ADAGIO: And throw the hay to the winds, lay your head in the shade, and your bum in the sun to sizzle. What more do you want?

MACABRE: On condition it's all done quickly, for money comes on one leg and leaves on a hundred! What scares me is ending up in the red, and Artie could burst in any minute now. You know how picayune he is! He wants everything in black and white!

ADAGIO: Why didn't that idiot go back where he came from, just like you told him in front of everybody in parliament?

GERTIE: Huh, not even a dog who followed a peasant's cart goes back to the farm if he's so much as licked a butcher's block in town. Much less Artie... and that's that! *(Exits.)*

ADAGIO: If there were as many epistles as there were apostles, a prophet would be hard put to be born!

MACABRE: Gertie says: "A hen will hatch ducklings, but she doesn't lay them!" You listen to her, because there's always more to her wisecracks than meets the eye. *(Exits.)*

ADAGIO: Hey, isn't Macabre a smart one! Every one of his words is pregnant—with at least twins and sometimes even triplets... all of them with curls. I bet everyone is worth between six months and sixteen years, according to circumstances. No matter which way you take them, they're always heavy.

GERTIE *(Enters):* How did you manage to get here in this blizzard?

ADAGIO: On a white horse.

GERTIE: Where did you manage to find ice and snow in August?

ADAGIO: The same place you found the blizzard!

GERTIE: And how did you find the big wide world in which we live?

ADAGIO: Well... In this big world
We call our house,
Everyone kowtows,
And everyone bows:

The mass to the class,
The class to the brass,
The brass to the ass,
And the ass to the grass!

GERTIE: Shhh!... speak a little softer. He may have left his ear under the threshold as he went out.

MACABRE *(Enters):* I forgot to tell you, Gertie! Carve up the sirloin and wrap it up in rhubarb leaves for him to take for bait! *(*GERTIE *goes off.)*

ADAGIO: All the meat to the foxes again?

MACABRE: To each his own, according to his merit!

EUGENE *(Enters and makes straight for* MACABRE*):* Please, sir, Eugene here.

MACABRE *(Pushes* Eugene *away):* Later, I don't have time now! *(*Eugene *bows and goes off.)*

ADAGIO: What about us, Macabre?

MACABRE: For the likes of you: bread!

ADAGIO: Well, I'm sorry, but I think you're wrong there. Man doesn't live on bread alone!

MACABRE: I know... when he has enough of it... but when it gets scarce, then you should see how man lives on hard, soured crusts! What do you say to that?

ADAGIO: I say: "Don't talk when your mouth is full."

MACABRE: You're forever chewing the cud!

ADAGIO: It's just that my mouth is full of pain, and I just can't swallow it.... And I don't dare spit out!

GERTIE *(Enters):* The beds are ready!

MACABRE: Come with me, Gertie, to tuck me in.... Will you?

GERTIE: Why not, Macabre? A woman is like water: where she's lain once, she'll come again.

MACABRE *(To* Adagio*):* And you, Adagio, remember: Don't spit in the pot you eat from! *(Starts off, but* Gertie *does not follow him.)*

ADAGIO: He doesn't give me much credit.

MACABRE: Why?

ADAGIO: I wasn't born yesterday! But now I think it's your turn to answer one of my questions! *(Approaches and swings a door, which squeaks.)* What is this door doing?

MACABRE: It's squeaking.

ADAGIO: Oil it, and it won't squeak.

MACABRE: Here, take it, you glutton, and have your fill! Let's go, Gertie. Why have you stopped halfway? You look at me as though I'll eat you up?

GERTIE: We won't eat up each other, that's for sure! But I'm afraid that the dark might swallow us both up?

MACABRE: There's a cure for that, too: let's have a candle! *(*Adagio *with a candle.)* Where are you going?!

ADAGIO: Why, to hold the candle for you, just like you said? *(*Macabre *goes off.)*

GERTIE *(To* Adagio*):* As soon as we get in, you blow it out! *(*Adagio *exits.)*

MACABRE *(Returns)*: Now I've had enough of him! *(Exits.)*

ADAGIO *(Returns)*: Listen, let's throw a blanket on him and beat him up! I'll go get the blanket! *(Exits.)*

MACABRE *(Returns)*: You blow out the candle, and I'll take him in hand. He'll be my trial balloon in the market; he's come along just in time! There hasn't been a better decoy in all history! He'll bring down eleven big mountains.

GERTIE: And dry up eleven bountiful fountains....

MACABRE: And when the slugs and worms start writhing in the sun, I'll just smile and wink at the road menders: roll your steam rollers over them and flatten out the ground! *(Exits.)*

GERTIE: Just you roll; everything good will die forever, but weeds will pop up again after the first rain!

ADAGIO *(Enters)*: When he doubles you up, you scream loud enough to deafen him! And be careful how you wriggle at your job; kick him with your heels down his back, enough to knock out his kidneys! *(Turns around.)* Are you coming, Macabre?

MACABRE *(Offstage)*: Like a calf to the slaughter! Baaaaaa!

EUGENE *(Enters)*: Moooo!

ADAGIO *(Shoves* EUGENE*)*: Later, we don't have time now!

EUGENE *(Obediently leaves)*: Moooo!

MACABRE *(Offstage)*: Baaaa!

GERTIE: I thought he'd get away at the last moment; now look at him: he's bleating! He won't show himself for anything!

MACABRE *(Offstage)*: Baaaaaaaa!

GERTIE: We'll fry his hide at tonight's meeting.

ADAGIO: It's damned tough, you can be sure! We'll have to cook it two or three times. *(Turns around.)* Are you coming soon, Macabre?

MACABRE *(Offstage)*: You go on ahead, I'll be right with you!

GERTIE: Just enough time to set up an ambush...come on! *(*GERTIE *and* ADAGIO *go off.)*

ARTIE *(Appears on the rostrum)*: This waaay! This waaaaay! This waaaay!

MACABRE *(Enters)*: Some pull that way, others pull this way...each pulls his own way, and the cart doesn't budge.

GERTIE *(Offstage)*: This waaaay! This waaaay! This waaaay!

ARTIE *(From the podium)*: This waaay! This way! This way!

MACABRE *(Does not know which way to turn)*: I'm coming. Wait a minute, till I get my bearings!

GERTIE *(Enters)*: What's the hitch this time?

MACABRE: I'm wanted urgently on the telephone. *(Goes off,* ARTIE *disappears from the rostrum.)*

ADAGIO *(Enters)*: They tease you and tease you! It's always like that...they hold out a morsel and just as you open your mouth to take a bite, it's jerked away!

GERTIE: You've got a cursed hand. Whoever you kill turns into a ghoul. *(Goes off, followed by* ADAGIO.*)*

ARTIE *(Appears on the rostrum)*: This waaaay! This waaay! This waaay!

MACABRE *(Enters):* Who was that, Son?

ARTIE: A traveler!

MACABRE: In other words: a human submarine!...a wandering vampire...a blood sucker! I just wonder what kind of fish he's trying to catch in these troubled waters of ours?

ARTIE: He got lost in the dark thick forest and wants us to give him quarters.

MACABRE: Quarter him then!

ARTIE: Six feet square, a little corner, he says.

MACABRE: He's lying!

ARTIE: There's no end to Asia!...and to integration...and to unconditional surrender, he says!

MACABRE: He's lying!

ARTIE: He says restoration! *Liberté, Égalité, Fraternité!*... Silk purses out of sows' ears! It's the twentieth century, he says....

MACABRE: Lies, all lies! He's a lying bastard!

ARTIE: Who the hell would know? Maybe he's asking for political asylum? I can't understand his language very well. It's neither left nor right.

MACABRE: Twelve percent, just in case...or, if it comes to the worst, a dime on the dollar! Our unselfish sense of oneness and our willingness to forget about insignificant slaughters—that's what it'll cost him. You tell him that, and I'm going to lie down. I feel like turning in.

GERTIE *(Offstage)*: This waaaay! This waaaay! Over here.

ARTIE *(Macabre starts to leave)*: Wait, Dad! *(Macabre halts)*

Have you forgotten the vows that we carved in sand?

MACABRE: How was that tune again? I forget it now?

ARTIE: When saints go marching out,
   Virtue at last cops out,
   And peasants become a little redder,
   We'll no longer be together!

MACABRE: Well, Son, it's either a rich life or death! Even if it is on credit! Grab what you can. Don't worry about repaying! But the installments keep accumulating!

ARTIE: That's how our vows stand, written in the sand!

MACABRE: Yes, that's how it stood once, as if carved in water, until we got squeezed from all sides! No more credit! No more vows! The water washed it away, and the wind blew it off!

ARTIE: I suppose some pretty wench erased it from your heart, Dad?

MACABRE: No, Artie, my son, no! It's because of strong winds and rough water that it's not worth making any vows. Everyone is forgiven for it!

ARTIE: Much is forgiven, Macabre, but nothing is ever forgotten! When you need it, up it comes!

MACABRE: So what if it does! Maybe it won't. Who can tell? One thing remains: you can't always live in fear of death! It's always better to die once and for all than to die a little each day and rot in life!

ARTIE: So you say, death is not the worst?

MACABRE: I only said that there are degrees to it!

ARTIE: Will you at least come to the funeral?

MACABRE: Yes, if you'll dig into your pockets for the taxi fare!

ARTIE: Maybe I can get time's chariot for us? *(Leaves the rostrum.)*

MACABRE: Wait a minute! I want to give them instructions on how to behave while we're away.

GERTIE *(Enters)*: If one of your cronies is making interventions again by telephone because of poor business, you can tell him from me that all of the most important seats in the quorum are already taken!

MACABRE: What if he offers us a fair swap?

GERTIE: Leave him alone, man. A beggar is no giver! *(Exits.)*

MACABRE: Fine, then, you cook an egg on the fire, break it in half, and, hot as it is, rub it on his nose!

ADAGIO *(Enters)*: What is this I hear? Are things tightening up again?

MACABRE: The bastard will never think of stealing eggs again! *(Exits.)*

ARTIE *(Appears on the rostrum)*: This waaaay! This waaaay! Hurry uphill, Macabre! Run! The taxi driver is impatient! He's cursing us with bell, book, and candle and wishing himself long life and good health at our expense!

MACABRE *(Enters):* The help here has gone to rack and ruin: they feed the cat, let the mice take over, and the cops go on shooting crap. They keep score with their billy-clubs—on the skin! They've lightened our purses, the motherland's breasts are dangling like empty bags, and hunger-maddened turkeys fly across the sky, like birds of doom!

ARTIE: If they carry on this way, they'll end up down the drain!

MACABRE *(Mounts the rostrum)*: I agree with that, unconditionally! *(*MACABRE *and* ARTIE *leave the rostrum.)*

ADAGIO *(Enters with* GERTIE*)*: What's all this? Wherever you look you see them reading psalms. Is it some saint's day today?

GERTIE: Yes. St. Pugnacius! If he should get into my bed just once, he'll be coming around more often. He'll turn his coat and change his vote. He'll leave that goat, or I'll cut his throat. *(Exits.)*

ADAGIO: Yeah, you could give him the works—but no matter how you heal the wounds, the scars will still remain. And, remember, there's no coat or cloak that'll hide a leper. No, we'll be damned till the end of our days!

HONEY *(Enters)*: What are you doing here at this time of the day?

ADAGIO: I'm spying on the spies, as it were. I watch you and you watch me, and whoever informs on the other first, he gets the merit. Hell, your left hand can't trust the right these days. Humanism's gone whacky! Everyone has started keeping tabs on everyone else. I'm sick of it; I wish I were far away from it all!

HONEY: Cool down, Adagio. The further you go, the closer to death you'll be. I think you're on your last legs.

ADAGIO: What about you, Cunty-Honey?

HONEY: I can't sleep a wink. I keep dreaming of mangy sheep in brambles. They sort of bleat.

ADAGIO: Like in heat!

HONEY: Maybe, I don't know. But I can clearly hear something smacking hungrily all night...as if walking through mud and minding its step. And I wish I could hear it here, in my heart, because I fear it would be over all too soon in my dream. Like Prince Charming and Cinderella. No sooner do I shut my eyes, than something like a film spreads over my eyes: like yellow paisley patterns, red fish bones, and a kind of pepper-and-salt color. And I keep waking, and even in my dream I keep an ear slightly ajar, to hear the weather forecast for the next classification period. *(Groaning and muttering.)* Shh...come, come...but on your tiptoes, so we don't scare him away. There he goes; now you see him, now you don't! *(Exits after the sound, followed by* ADAGIO.*)*

ARTIE *(Appears on the rostrum)*: They'll be playing cards all night! All kinds of them: Punch cards! Credit cards! Party cards!

MACABRE *(Appears on the rostrum)*: And there'll be stars galore! Shooting stars! Generals' stars! Film stars! Water will gush upon the sand!

ARTIE: Chains will clank upon the concrete. And, out of the walls of fortresses, mother's milk will continue oozing for centuries to come! *(Both disappear from the rostrum.)*

HONEY *(Enters)*: Who is it? Who shattered people's dreams?

ADAGIO *(Enters)*: The juggler!

HONEY: Do you mean Macabre?

ADAGIO: I'm not suggesting anyone. No names have been mentioned! All I know is that he juggled with dreams just like a juggler tossing plates in a circus. So long as his hands were firm, the magic worked.

HONEY: And the mouth moved up to the top of the head! And, all at once, everybody started talking through his hat!

ADAGIO: And their eyes got too big for their heads! And they gazed at the stars, and suddenly everyone stopped saving. The few remaining monuments are pissed on by dogs...and the janitor rolled off the roof into the septic pit, from which a snake, yellow as an egg, crawled out!

HONEY: And their noses dropped down to their chins! And everyone's hair started growing out of his eyebrows, as if the fashion had come for low brows and high asses. *(Exits.)*

ADAGIO: The thumb, too, as I told you at the beginning, slipped under the index, and two fingers on the map are like two thousand miles on the earth. The pilgrims wore their feet to a nub and never got anywhere. And so...and so...they held on grimly, breathing as their last words: we are near, almost there. And drunken dreams grimaced in warped mirrors, until his hand shook. *(*HONEY *enters.)*

HONEY: Whose, the juggler's?

ADAGIO: I'm not insinuating anyone. No names have been mentioned. All I know is that the mirror fell on the stone...and shattered. Now nobody knows how to put together the shattered dream, so everyone lives piecemeal....Get what you can!

HONEY: Would you sing something nice and sensible so that I can fall asleep on your shoulder?

ADAGIO: How do you pay?

HONEY: In kind, according to the service rendered...since nowadays no one will do anything without payment. All right, get on with it! But if you've ever lighted a cigarette, you'll know that it's useless to start puffing before the match is fully aflame. Don't be impatient, the flame might just flare up and immediately go out.

ADAGIO *(Music for Sexual Act.* ADAGIO *sings):* There was a fat gal named Honey...

HONEY: Easy, easy, don't burn me up!

ADAGIO: Whose past was far from sunny...

HONEY: Keep that up and I'm through!

ADAGIO: She spat on the floor...

HONEY: I can hardly wait!

ADAGIO: And swore like a whore...

HONEY: My cup runneth over!

ADAGIO: Now its fun-on-the-run Honey-Cunty!

HONEY: Sing it, Sam!

ADAGIO: Honey-Cunty, Cunty-Honey!

HONEY: Just a little more. Go on! *(*ADAGIO *stops singing; the music ceases.)* Why did you? Why? Why did you stop just now?

ADAGIO: I like to tease you, Cunty-Honey.

HONEY: So that's the thanks I get for having brought you from rags to riches overnight!

ADAGIO: You mean to the gallows!

HONEY: You know what happens to slimy characters. I'll kill you!

ADAGIO: I'm not the kind of man that women could kill with their charms. *(Exits.)*

HONEY: If you're going to sell me out, I'd rather you kill me with your own hands! *(Goes off after ADAGIO.)*

ARTIE *(Enters carrying GERTIE in his arms)*: I like white, Gertie. Your white body! *(Sets GERTIE down on her feet.)*

GERTIE: Yes, but white may also be forbidding in its purity. Just don't get the wrong idea, Artie! You don't dare touch it for fear of getting it dirty! *(ARTIE throws her down on the ground.)*

MACABRE *(Appears on the rostrum)*: You know what the smell of a white oleander blossom is like, Son? *(ARTIE starts. GERTIE flees.)* At first it's delighting and exciting, but afterwards your head feels like bursting! *(Disappears from the rostrum.)*

ARTIE: The crimson poppy in the glare of the sun blinds you! And the six-petalled field flower makes you vomit! Whatever is beautiful can do you harm! Gertie, where did you go? I need you! Where are you?! *(Exits.)*

ADAGIO *(Enters with HONEY)*: Kill yourself, yourself!

HONEY: My heart is torn and bleeding, Adagio. At least comfort me.

ADAGIO: Comfort today, comfort tomorrow. Every day you just want to come fart, no wonder your heart is torn apart!

HONEY: Even a priest's cassock can get torn. Never mind people's reputation! Everything gets patched up and mended. The main thing is that it lasts.

ADAGIO: Nothing lasts forever.

HONEY: I know that better than anyone.

ADAGIO: What do you know?

HONEY: I know that even green wood burns along with the dry wood.

ADAGIO: What's that? What's that?

HONEY: You can't feed a bonfire with sawdust, that's what...*(Cries.)*

ADAGIO: What are you crying for? Wait, think about it: and loosen your girdle a little! *(Strip tease.)*

HONEY: Eh!

ADAGIO: Fill your lungs with fresh air; it'll bolster you up!

HONEY: Ah!

ADAGIO: Relax! Your straps are biting into your shoulders!

HONEY: Oh!

ADAGIO: And loosen the laces on your girdle by a few inches. *(*HONEY *ends up with nothing on. For how long? That's up to the director.)* Now do you see? No use lecturing a hungry man about food; rather give him something to bite into...like this!

HONEY: Quite true! With no clothes on, I do breathe much more freely, naked like this!

ADAGIO: Like the naked truth.

HONEY: The ugly truth.

ADAGIO: The easily accessible truth.

EUGENE *(Enters)*: Moooo! Moooo!

ADAGIO *(Pushes* EUGENE *away)*: Later, I don't have time now! *(*EUGENE *bows and leaves obediently.)*

EUGENE: Mooooo!

HONEY: Take me, if it's like you said just now. Match your words with deeds!

ADAGIO: You're sure looking for trouble. You want to let the wolf guard your sheep!

HONEY: It's not trousers that makes a man!

ADAGIO: In any case we'll leave it as arranged. But tell me first, without any rush or nervousness, I really am curious to know: if someone doesn't want you, won't you yourself lure someone into your embrace after I've gone my own way?

HONEY: Yes, my dear, here they say that what a woman slaughters for meat is bound to be uneatable.

ADAGIO: And you put a pestle between your legs and hold it there while you kill your chickens!

HONEY *(Sobs)*: There indeed would be meat, but it wouldn't be so sweet! I'd rather nestle or wrestle than squeeze a pestle!

ADAGIO: Go ahead and cry! When you wake up from your love dreams, it'll become quite clear to you, Cunty-Honey, that man is man and woman is woman, and ever the twain shall have meat!

HONEY: All meat goes the way of our life hopes and illusions—to the dogs.

ADAGIO: Yes, but the pot remains!

HONEY: What's the use if it's licked clean! Today it no longer matters...but once upon a time!

ADAGIO: You asked your mother what you'd be!

HONEY: Oh, for heaven's sake, don't start that now! What's over is over and done with!

ADAGIO: Oh, do tell me, why the hell not! You'll make Macabre pay for it through the nose once he's down! *(Starts to leave.)* He'll stone for his own sins and ours, too! Come over and take a peek! Shhh! Gertie is carrying on diplomatic relations in bed with him! *(ADAGIO and HONEY go off.)*

MACABRE *(MACABRE enters carrying GERTIE in his arms)*: Why should other people's happiness distract us from our own despair? For how long are we going to look as if we live for other people's progress? *(Pushes GERTIE down on her feet.)*

GERTIE: I don't know, Macabre; but even if I knew, I wouldn't be believed, because it's up to you to decide. All I have to do is keep clear of any perversity! Because you're just great!

MACABRE: Tell me, now, tell me honestly: am I clever? *(Enter HONEY and ADAGIO.)*

ADAGIO: Your intellect shines down upon us like the sun!

MACABRE: Tell me, now, tell me without beating around the bush: am I popular?

HONEY: The goodness of your heart is only matched by the splendor of your soul! The world worships the wisdom of your words! *(HONEY and ADAGIO exit.)*

MACABRE: And what about my strength? Tell me without embellishment, is it declining?

GERTIE: You're terrific, Macabre! You're certainly still very strong!

MACABRE: And you're pretty!

GERTIE: You're rich, too!

MACABRE: And you're raw! I'll have to invest some capital in you to see some returns on raw material.

GERTIE: The beauty of my body comes to me from my father and mother, and there is nothing anyone can do about it. Even when I have given what you are yearning after, Macabre, it'll still remain my own! *(*Macabre *throws her on the ground.)*

ARTIE *(Appears on the rostrum)*: Cold memories conceal their fingers under other people's hearts. They're all lying to you because they hate you, but I'm your son! I both love you and hate you. I both want you and don't want you. I'll tell you, though: if it's true that history is our teacher, then the teacher is the only one that you should lie with, because only her children live forever!

MACABRE: I'm sick of my power! And I'm sick of sycophants! I'm not going to keep running after my desires like a greyhound after a mechanical rabbit. Gertie, where are you? I want you!

ARTIE: No use looking for her. She'll smother you with the charms of her everyday banalities and inanities!

MACABRE: Gertie, where are you?

ARTIE: No good looking for her, I told you! She's a young thing. Even if you could understand her, what good is it to you, if you, old as you are, can't keep up with her? The frustration will kill you!

MACABRE: Gertie, where are you? I waaaaant you! *(*Macabre *exits.)*

ARTIE: They'll all lying to you because they hate you, but I'm your soooon! I both love you and haaate you! Oh, you specter with vicious serpents oozing fire instead of milk! Oh, you monster! Are you going to pour the venom of your lust over my father?! *(Disappears from the rostrum.)*

EUGENE *(Runs across the stage)*: Mooooo!

ADAGIO *(Enters with* HONEY*)*: We'll become famous by dragging him through the mud after he's dead.

HONEY: Yes, we'll alter his past until it's tailored to suit us!

ADAGIO: But leave wide seams, because a man has a way of growing and filling out. Everything becomes too small for him!

HONEY: No, I still won't do it!

ADAGIO: You don't dare!

HONEY: Even if I don't dare, it's still your fault. I smell a conspiracy between the brass and the class. Their collusion causes constant confusion! Remember, Adagio, you've got to keep in with God and the rod if you want to get a return on your wad...and that's what's most important of all. So what are you waiting for? Why hesitate? Go ahead!

ADAGIO: I'm not hesitating, just being cautious. I want to catch up with my fortune, but I'm careful not to run past it in my hurry.

HONEY: Are you going to start doing anything before the autumn rains? Hurry, man, life is short!

ADAGIO: I will, but I want you to tell me...tell me about your secret-most self, concealed right at the bottom, that only belongs to you!

HONEY: Wouldn't you like to know?

ADAGIO: Speak up, then!

HONEY: Look how impudent he is! Go away then, go!

ADAGIO: Who, me?

HONEY: How many times have I told you not to sit on my desk in my office when a stranger calls!

ADAGIO: Aren't we kind of family?

HONEY: Familiarity breeds contempt. We can't have that sort of thing going on at work! Otherwise you'd be throwing paper clips into my neckline in front of everybody, wouldn't you? Or making paper darts out of top secret files? Or rummaging through my handbag in front of the whole staff? Or ramming your cigarette into my mouth? Or making balloons out of contraceptives and leaning across six rows of chairs to tap them against my bottom—while I'm making a speech, no less!

ADAGIO: I did it out of boredom, without any ulterior motives!

HONEY: Well, I don't tolerate any familiarity or vulgarity which you assume in order to show the crowds that you are in with the V.I.P.'s. And in the end you'll be cruelly punished for it, just like any old flunkey! Once he's done his job he gets a kick in the ass! Go away!

ADAGIO: How? On foot?

HONEY: Take the Rolls-Royce.

ADAGIO: It's hardly possible, milady! The chauffeur has his day off today!

HONEY: Oh, don't be a fool! You ought to be given a good whipping!

ADAGIO: Mummy's going to whip me!

HONEY: I'm not wet behind the ears. You're not going to take me for a ride. Get out of here, d'you hear me? All right, I forgive you, you big boob! Clear out now, you nincompoop! Scram! I don't want you near me! *(Pushes him toward the edge of the tower.)* You've just upset me, I can hardly breathe; Beat it now, before I kick you!

ADAGIO *(Resists)*: You want me dead, do you? *(Springs away from her.)* O.K., then, thanks for your neighborly solicitude! I'll go without your help, but the other way!

HONEY: Do you at least know where you'll be going?

ADAGIO: I'll follow my nose!

HONEY: To the East?

ADAGIO: Into life!

HONEY: To the West?

ADAGIO: As far away from here as possible! *(Runs toward the first passage.)*

THE SEVEN MAIDS *(They block the first passage):* Come! Come!

ADAGIO: Farther, still farther! *(Takes a step back, then rushes to the second passage.)*

THE SEVEN MAIDS *(They move away from the first passage to block the second one)*: Come! Come!

ADAGIO: Farther, as far away as possible! *(Takes a step back, then rushes to the third passage.)*

THE SEVEN MAIDS *(They move away from the second and block the third passage):* Come on! Come on!

ADAGIO *(Runs back)*: I'm surrounded! Encircled with red ink!

HONEY: Ha, ha, ha, ha, ha!

ADAGIO: Honey, I've stepped into the trap which I laid myself! You told me that I was setting up a trap for someone else!

HONEY: Ha, ha, ha, ha, ha! *(HONEY exits.)*

ADAGIO: You can have the sirloin! And the bait! Take the snare off my feet! And the weight off my mind! And the veil from my eyes! And the blot off my record! And the stripes off my sleeve! I'm content with dry bread! Life means more to me than the standard of living!

HONEY *(Offstage)*: Ha, ha, ha, ha, ha!

ADAGIO: From now on I'll obey you blindly, Honey...you give the orders! Humiliate me as much as you want! I'm no longer a man...arf, arf, arf! *(Exits like a dog.)*

HONEY *(Offstage)*: Ha, ha, ha, ha, ha!

MACABRE *(Enters with* ARTIE*)*: What does she find so funny tonight?

ARTIE: Tickle-tickle!

HONEY *(Offstage)*: Ha, ha, ha, ha, ha!

MACABRE: I wouldn't say so, judging by the sound. . .tickle-tickle is tinkling. . .like a bell. . . .

HONEY: *(Offstage)*: Ha, ha, ha, ha, ha!

MACABRE: That sound could be caused by gas pains. *(*ARTIE *starts to leave.)* Where are you going?

ARTIE: I'm going to ask them if they can carry on their argument across the fence in a more civilized manner! *(Exits.)*

MACABRE: O.K., but come around afterwards to check if my blanket is still on me! *(Lies down and covers himself.)*

HONEY *(Offstage)*: Ha, ha, ha, ha, ha!

ADAGIO *(Enters)*: How am I going to escape? Someplace where no one will think of looking for me. What about the wardrobe! *(Rushes toward the wardrobe.)*

ARTIE *(From the wardrobe)*: Occupied!

ADAGIO: Now you see, Adagio, what it is not to make the necessary reservation! But I know where I'll go! I'll shove Macabre under the bed and I'll get into his own place! *(Drags* MACABRE *off the bed, onto the floor, and under the bed. Gets into bed himself.)* When I pull the blankets over my head, not even my own mother will recognize me! *(Covers himself.)*

HONEY *(Enters)*: Ha, ha, ha, ha, ha! My dream bust is a bust dream!

ARTIE *(Enters)*: Everything looked much better while I was still able to retreat, but now. . .now it looks as if the die's been cast. An epoch is smashed on a diceboard. You ask me if I'm afraid? I'm half dead with fear! And I have no more choice.

HONEY: Don't be stingy, and it'll come true. It's unlucky to be tight-fisted!

ARTIE: What brings bad luck is a busybody pestering you with good advice!

HONEY: You pay someone from outside to get rid of him, and there'll be time for you to insult me. There's still a lot of haggling to be done. But this thing I told you, it'll come out cheaper in the end, and you won't have to dirty your hands.

ARTIE: But we should also make a showing in the community. We should prove that the Almighty's grace has passed from the mighty to the mightier, as prophesied.

HONEY: So, it means both: the crime in public and the public in crime. What matters is to save face...although there are even some who don't mind cutting off their nose to spite their face. Rather that than face the wall!

ARTIE: And with mourning widows behind the wall, planted on brass bedsteads, as in school books...sniffing and humming the "Marseillaise," as though they were about to lay an egg.

HONEY: As you so rightly pointed out: it's the present beat generation that tomorrow will lead the nation...."Make love, not War!" *(Starts off.)*

ARTIE: Wait, don't go! *(She stops.)* It's late, Cunty-Honey!

HONEY: Too late to add insult to injury! *(Starts off.)*

ARTIE: Wait, Honey, don't go! *(She stops.)* I've already instructed the constable how to force the rejoicing in the public squares!

HONEY: Let them strike up military marches and deadly classics, with announcements during the intervals that something very important will happen but that not much notice should be taken of all that. So, the matter is an urgent one, but not such as to give rise to anxiety. In other words, it is a life and death issue, but there is no need to worry or hurry.

ARTIE: Except that janitors are becoming landlords and vice-versa. Barbers and those who are shaved...vice-versa and opposite of the other way around. The higher you fly, the harder you fall. And polluted market places are ploughed up by troubleshooters harnessed to the plough instead of oxen!

HONEY: What about the oxen?

ARTIE: They have the day off.

HONEY: And Macabre?

ARTIE: Death for the old and feeble! At last we've come to the crux of the matter! There, we'll kill him according to our ancient custom.

HONEY: Will he go to the ritual?

ARTIE: Like sheep to the congress!

HONEY: He's like the man who sows the wind—he always hopes that the whirlwind might change direction!

ARTIE: I'm now going to issue last instructions...Gertie!

GERTIE *(Enters)*: I'm sorry I'm so late. I would have come much earlier, but some eunuch called Eugene stopped me. Do you know *it*?

ARTIE: You mean *her*?

HONEY: No, *him*!

GERTIE: Well then, what sex does *it* belong to?

HONEY: Middling: neither here nor there, always in the middle. Whatever happens, he's always placed right. You do as you like, but I'll take care of him. It may be important in the future.

ARTIE: I should never have overlooked him! We met so many times at different places, yet I never cultivated him. I thought he was just a local yokel. Thanks for the tip. I'll send him my visiting card with expressions of my highest esteem...and you, Gertie, wash his feet on my behalf...and walk his shoes around the table...offer him full comfort! *(She starts to leave.)* Wait, I haven't finished dictating. At the crack of dawn, make some corn-bread for Macabre's death ritual. What are you waiting for?

GERTIE: Initial it here so we know who dictated. All I do is to put things down—you're the dictator! *(Exits.)*

ARTIE: What bothers me now is that fellow Eugene.

HONEY: You're right. Things aren't so simple.

ARTIE: Are you trying to frighten me?

HONEY: I'm trying to cover you from all sides, because a riddle is a riddle, like an embryo in a mother's womb.

ARTIE: Do you find it hard to make up your mind?

HONEY: No, never!

ARTIE: Give me proof or I'll write you off!

HONEY: I'll get the seven maids who've never been laid, in their petticoats inside out, to keep watch around the house all night!

ARTIE: Let them say anathema.

HONEY: Is that when you address all kinds of oaths, threats, and accusations at someone, but fail to state his name?

ARTIE: That's it, Cunty-Honey! Frightening propaganda! Whether you like it or not! As they say: the situation is unclear and gives cause for utmost caution, which in turn calls for quiescence. So, as I said, I'm going to take a walk around the lobbies in the hope of bumping into Eugene! *(Exits.)*

HONEY: It seems to me that confusion has grown. Artie is whistling in the dark, and his flanks are unprotected. All he needs is a prod. Hey you! What're you waiting for? Where's your atmosphere of mutual respect, notwithstanding misunderstandings and disagreement on an insignificant part of the issue? *(*Artie *goes off. Music.)*

THE SEVEN MAIDS AND GERTIE *(Sing and act out a ceremony of Anathema—the weird dance of damnation):*

> Molly mocks
> Prickly pricks
> Kooky cock,
> Someone sticks.
> Knock, knock!

ADAGIO *(Peers from beneath the blanket):* Who's there?
THE SEVEN MAIDS AND GERTIE:

> High and mighty,
> High and mighty!

GERTIE: I'm a specter with vicious dragons!
THE SEVEN MAIDS AND GERTIE:

> Molly mocks
> Prickly pricks.
> Kooky cock,
> Someone sticks.
> Knock, knock!

ADAGIO *(Peers from beneath the blanket):* Who's there?
THE SEVEN MAIDS AND GERTIE:

> High and mighty,
> High and mighty!

GERTIE: Kiss them, and you'll see they're the only breasts which give fire instead of milk!
ADAGIO: Would you say that it's a court messenger's fault that the scales of justice are weighted with lead on the side of the rulers? Have you ever known a ship to sail in spittle? I'm not going to spit.

What the hell am I, an earthling, doing here among you fairies? Why are you picking on me?

GERTIE: Because the rain-dancers, until yesterday gaily kicking their heels in boudoirs, are now croaking in swamps! Snow frills in the ditches but can only cover the mountains! Because what's big is big, whether it's hot or cold...whether it's white or black...whether by hook or by crook.

THE SEVEN MAIDS AND GERTIE:

> Molly mocks
> Prickly pricks,
> Kooky cock,
> Someone sticks.
> Knock, knock!

ADAGIO *(Peers from beneath the blanket):* Who's there again?
THE SEVEN MAIDS AND GERTIE:

> High and mighty,
> High and mighty!

ADAGIO: Look, what angels!...And I have to go tomfooling with a tomboy like Gertie!

ARTIE *(Enters):* Where's Adagio? *(*THE SEVEN MAIDS *and* GERTIE *exit.)*

HONEY *(Enters):* Adagio is in my bedside table. And Eugene?

ARTIE: He's completely vanished, but maybe he's hatching something—I'll have to stop him! *(Comes to the bed.)* Macabre, it's time for you to take off your mask! Throw off the blanket!

ADAGIO *(From beneath the blanket)*: I dare not tell you the truth...I can't, either; my eyes smart from the bright light. What is it that keeps shining from the river?

HONEY: It's the reflection of faraway lightning.

ARTIE: Like your former glory.

THE SEVEN MAIDS *(Off stage)*: Better stalemate than checkmate, better peace than police, better right than might, better...

ADAGIO: Hear it rolling, hear it rolling...thundering...

HONEY: All hell has broken loose! The earth is thirsting for justice! Get up!

ADAGIO: I can't. I feel as if I'm drunk.

ARTIE: You're drunk from boredom, Macabre! To hell with you! *(Exits.)*

ADAGIO: And a current, my good friends. I feel a current in my body, as if ants were crawling all over me. Take off the electrodes. And you, Cunty-Honey, come to me. I feel sad....Come lie next to me!

HONEY: I won't, Macabre, because you're sad out of spite! There are also other reasons.

ADAGIO: What reasons are those?

HONEY: You'll drown and yet there'll be no flood! *(Exits.)*

ADAGIO: I'm yearning for freedom!

GERTIE *(Enters bringing cornbread)*: Well, you can't buy freedom in the market place! *(*ARTIE *comes in wearing a butcher's apron.* GERTIE *speaks to* ARTIE*)* Here's the cornbread.

ARTIE: Put it on his head!

ADAGIO: Don't bring anything to me! Go away! I'm not hungry! Shoo! Scat!

GERTIE *(To* ARTIE*)*: He wants to die contemptuous of life!

ARTIE: But I don't want to live appreciative of death! Put it on his head, before Eugene comes to mess things up!

ADAGIO: What are you trying to do, Gertie? You, too, Gertie?

HONEY *(Enters carrying an axe, which she hands to* ARTIE*)*: Strike while the cornbread is hot! *(Exits.)*

ADAGIO: Where I expected the sun to shine on me, I got an axe on the head instead! *(*ARTIE *hits him on the head with the axe through the cornbread.)* Gertie! You, too, my lovely...my sweet ...(ARTIE *hits him again, he sways and falls on the floor by the bed.)*

ARTIE: I'm not responsible for your death, Macabre. The cornbread is what killed you! *(Throws away the axe and exits.* GERTIE *exits on the other side of the stage.)*

MACABRE *(Drags himself out from under the bed.)* Was that for me? *(Enter* HONEY. MACABRE *goes up to her.)* You're killing with boredom...suffocating with red tape! You're killing indiscriminately whatever positive trend you manage to lay your hands on!

ADAGIO *(Revives)*: They've killed all that's human in me. Arf, arf, arf! *(Falls back again.)*

MACABRE: And you even forget to advise me by postcard of the train of events! What are you thinking?

HONEY: We ourselves don't know anymore what to think. It looks as if your soul has hardened inside you.

MACABRE: Ha! I'll have to take a purgative. . . *(Exits followed by* HONEY.*)*

ARTIE *(Enters with* GERTIE*)*: My hands are clean. Try now, Gertie, with all due pomp and honors to remove him from public life as soon as possible and get him off the political scene. But you must watch your step. We're not yet quite clear about Eugene. Do the job according to the system of thin air.

GERTIE: As they say: watered down.

ARTIE: Yes. . .so that we get the spirit of the message between the lines. Jot it down if you find it hard to remember. The bully that beats up your bull is a hero! And, if you get a few hours overtime on this job, put it down in your notebook. You'll get fifty percent, only hurry up! But if Eugene arrives unexpectedly, act dumb. I'm going to rifle the works to get some ideas! *(Exits.)*

GERTIE *(After* ARTIE*)*: People know this very well, Artie! Where might is master, justice is its handmaiden. It's better to keep your mouth shut. We don't have to pour water over an extinguished fire! *(Exits.)*

MACABRE *(Enters with* HONEY*)*: All this trouble. . .

HONEY: A cannonball. . .

MACABRE: Yes. . .just to kill a sparrow. What a comedown!

GERTIE *(Enters)*: A ghost! *(Swoons.* HONEY *catches her. At the same moment,* ARTIE *enters and rushes to the bed where* ADAGIO *is lying dead.)*

MACABRE *(To* HONEY*)*: What's the matter with her? What did she say?

HONEY: All she said was, "The mindless fool sells wisdom". . .and she died of fright!

GERTIE *(Revives)*: You've killed my personality. . .Ga, ga, ga!. . . *(Collapses.)*

ARTIE: Well, cornbread is what killed poor Adagio!

ADAGIO: Arf, arf, arf!

MACABRE: It's only the poor man that's killed by cornbread, Son.

GERTIE: Ga, ga, ga!

ARTIE *(Swoons):* Taxes impoverish everyone, Father...*(Drops to the floor;* HONEY *supports him.)*

MACABRE *(To* HONEY*)*: What did he say?

HONEY: All he said was, "When the horse is dead, everyone knows the right cure." And he died of failure!

ARTIE *(Revives for a minute)*: You've killed all that's beautiful in me...*(Collapses.)*

THE SEVEN MAIDS:

> Molly mocks
> Prickly pricks.
> Kooky cock,
> Someone sticks.
> Knock, knock!

MACABRE: Who's there?

EUGENE *(Enters)*: Eugene!

MACABRE *(Shoves him away):* Later, I haven't time now! *(*EUGENE *bows servilely and leaves.)*

HONEY: Do you realize what you've done, Macabre! For heaven's sake, that was Eugene!

THE SEVEN MAIDS *(General confusion)*:

> High and mighty,
> High and mighty!

HONEY *(Leaves and everyone in confusion rushes after her)*: Eugene, come back! Wait! Wait, don't go! Let there be peace among the mighty! *(Only* ARTIE *remains on stage, acting the part of a monument.)*

ACT II: HALTER

(Everything as in Act I, except for ARTIE'S *statue under canvas. Nightmarish confusion.)*

THE SEVEN MAIDS *(Singing and dancing)*:

> Words are wasted on the dead,
> Try to praise the quick instead.
> Gold and dollar are the same.
> Never mind the country's fame!
> Every shepherd feeds his herd.
> Leaders could, too, if they cared!

(They exit.)

ADAGIO *(Henceforth acts as a dog)*: How are we to look dignified on an empty stomach! An empty sock can't stand upright!

EUGENE *(Enters)*: Fetch!

ADAGIO *(Comes to him quickly)*: Arf-arf-arf-arf! *(Gets a lump of sugar.)*

GERTIE (Henceforth acts as a goose): Our schools can't be very good, since those in charge of them send their children to parochial schools!

EUGENE: Goosie-goosie!

GERTIE *(Gabbles)*: Ga-ga-ga-ga-ga! *(Gets a tidbit from* EUGENE.*)*

ADAGIO: He who uses other's people's money to build his fortune will soon be dragging stones to the political graveyard!

EUGENE: Fetch!

ADAGIO: Arf-arf-arf-arf!

GERTIE: Too many cooks spoil the broth!

EUGENE: Goosie-goosie!

GERTIE: Ga-ga-ga-ga-ga!

ADAGIO: A warm coat on your back is worth a million hot words on paper!

EUGENE: Fetch!

ADAGIO: Arf-arf-arf-arf-arf!

GERTIE: I wonder who looks after the governess' children?

EUGENE: Goosie-goosie!

GERTIE: Ga-ga-ga-ga!

ADAGIO: The only remedy against mass drowning is for the masses to learn how to swim!

EUGENE: Fetch!

ADAGIO: Arf-arf-arf-arf-arf!

GERTIE: What's the good of propaganda's pearl necklaces if they're meant to strangle you!

EUGENE: Goosie-goosie!

GERTIE: Ga-ga-ga-ga!

ADAGIO: We've wised up: foreign economic aid feeds you with the spoon and gouges your eyes with the handle!

EUGENE: Fetch!

ADAGIO: Arf-arf-arf-arf!

GERTIE: That's why it's better to give up halfway than to keep going along the wrong road to everlasting failure!

EUGENE: Goosie-goosie!

GERTIE: Ga-ga-ga-ga!

ADAGIO: Because a poor society spends little but costs a lot!

EUGENE: Fetch!

ADAGIO: Arf-arf-arf-arf!

GERTIE: Humph, wise men tell others how to work, but they're wise enough not to work themselves!

EUGENE: Goosie-goosie!

GERTIE: Ga-ga-ga-ga!

ADAGIO: But what good is it when one's career is never quite enough!

EUGENE: Fetch! Goosie-goosie! *(All three hide on the stage when they hear someone coming.)*

MACABRE *(Comes in hunched over and shuffling.* HONEY *helps him along.)* Honey, I still haven't been able to figure out why we're chasing after that Eugene?

HONEY: You're slow in catching on.

MACABRE: At my age, I'm lucky to be catching at all!

HONEY: We'll still have to go more to the right.

MACABRE: There's an abyss to the right!

HONEY: No, there isn't. Your bearings are all wrong. *(Starts off.)*

ADAGIO *(Barks at them)*: Arf-arf-arf-arf!

HONEY *(To* MACABRE*):* Let's go; why've you stopped?

ADAGIO: Arf-arf-arf-arf!

MACABRE: Don't you hear how he's barking!

ADAGIO: Arf-arf-arf-arf!

HONEY: His bite is worse than his bark. Get away! *(*ADAGIO *sits down.* HONEY *and* MACABRE *start off, but now* GERTIE *attacks them.)*

GERTIE: Sssss! Sssss! Sssss!

MACABRE: Hey, tease, stop it, please!

HONEY: She teases when she pleases!

GERTIE: Ssss! Sssss! Sssss!

MACABRE: Her tease gives me no peace!

HONEY: You don't hear good, Macabre. That's a goose! Shooo! *(*GERTIE *exits.)* And don't jump at every sound! You'll loosen your screws!

MACABRE: At my age what's one screw, more or less?

HONEY: Your nerves are shot, lean on me! *(They exit.)*

THE SEVEN MAIDS *(An orgy in song and dance)*:

> Legs run around,
> Feet beat the ground.
> Behinds shake about,
> And bellies stick out.
> And souls quake,
> Backbones break!
> Hearts will bleed—
> There's no need!
> Pfft!

(They dance out.)

MACABRE *(Enters with* HONEY*)*: And what's that sticking out there?

HONEY: The reapers are reaping.

MACABRE: What are they reaping?

HONEY: You know what you sowed.

MACABRE: Discord?

HONEY: Uh-huh. And now people are spitting at each other, shitting on each other, and hitting each other.

MACABRE: But it seems to me that they're biting off more than they can chew!

HONEY: You don't see good.

EUGENE *(Enters):* Please, sir, Eugene here....

MACABRE *(Pushes him):* Later, I don't have time now! *(Eugene bows and leaves.)* Wait! What did he say his name was?

HONEY: A common one; he doesn't warrant attention. *(*EUGENE *returns.)*

MACABRE: Didn't he say: "Eugene?"

EUGENE: Yes, "Eugene."

HONEY: He said: "Routine."

EUGENE: Yes, "Eugene."

HONEY: He said: "Guillotine."

EUGENE: Yes, "Eugene."

HONEY: He said: "A rude teen."

MACABRE: And I would interpret what he said as: "Eugene."

HONEY: You don't interpret very well. Lean on me. *(They start off.)*

ADAGIO *(Barks at them):* Arf-arf-arf-arf!

HONEY: And be careful where you walk; you stepped on his tail! *(They leave.)*

ADAGIO: Arf-arf-arf-arf!

GERTIE: What is this I hear, that you're a dog?

ADAGIO: Yes, unfortunately. What about you?

GERTIE: It depends. Throughout history they have given me or taken away from me all kinds of properties.

ADAGIO: Why, I had a lot of different treatments, too. We have the same fate.

GERTIE: I was all sorts of things—just imagine! A fox—sly, and a skylark—gay, and a caterpillar—crawly...and now I'm a goose: Now I'm a complete fool...Ga-ga-ga-ga!

ADAGIO: And I used to be a billy goat: wild and strong-headed...Baaaa-baaa! And later in my heyday, a wild boar: passionate and ferocious...Grrr-grrr!. Those are also my happiest memories of the time I sowed my wild oats. All the rest is thin and pale. It almost faded out completely when I was a worm, a catfish, a chameleon, and so forth.

GERTIE: Why, how many faces do you have?

ADAGIO: I don't even know myself! At first I kept a record. I hoped to be able to pay back the debt, but soon I lost both the accounts and every hope.

GERTIE: And, as for me, from cherry-red dreams, I cooked an ideological jam.

ADAGIO: In my case, I think the decisive factor in everything was the large traffic in my spiritual domicile. Not a single change passed me by.

GERTIE: At least you've never had a dull moment.

ADAGIO: There's almost no spice I haven't been seasoned with. But I tried with all my might. I was always fired up! But still I never succeeded in being a man.

GERTIE: They say that pride is what adorns a man.

ADAGIO: I've heard that, though I've never come across it.

GERTIE: Well, real men are rare.

ADAGIO: And they say that they're characterized by wisdom.

GERTIE: Yes, so they insist, but I don't understand why at the same time there's twice as much talk about human stupidity.

THE SEVEN MAIDS *(Come in from all sides):* About scientific idiocy!

ADAGIO: About human obtuseness!

THE SEVEN MAIDS: About unnatural materialism!

GERTIE: About drastic humanism!

THE SEVEN MAIDS: About sexual imperialism!

ADAGIO: About infanticidal aestheticism!

EUGENE *(Enters):* Fetch! *(*THE MAIDS *go off.)*

ADAGIO: Arf-arf! *(To* GERTIE.*)* Pardon me for a moment, my master is calling.

EUGENE: Goosie-goosie! *(Exits.)*

GERTIE: And mine is calling me, too.

ADAGIO: Maybe we're fellow-treavellers. What's your master's name?

GERTIE: I don't know. But, at this particular moment, that's not of historical importance.

ADAGIO: Absolutely right. I don't know the identity of mine, either. And what does yours do?

GERTIE: Who knows?

ADAGIO: Mine is an enigmatic personality, too.

GERTIE: A gray eminence.

ADAGIO: A figure cast to the forefront by enigmatic coincidence. Scumfloats. But let's hurry to report before our master gets lost on the foggy horizon. Arf-arf! *(Exists.)*

GERTIE: Ga-ga! *(Exits.)*

HONEY *(Enters):* Things are developing as well as could be desired.

EUGENE *(Enters):* Please, Eugene here...

HONEY *(Shoves him):* Later, I don't have time now!

EUGENE: But when you do have...just wait! Then I'll be the one who has no time.

HONEY: First of all, you're invented, but not for me!

EUGENE: I am Eugene.

HONEY: Why, you don't even exist.

EUGENE: What do you mean I don't exist, when I'm Eugene!

HONEY: Don't lie to me when I'm the one who thought you up!

EUGENE: My sweet little mommy!

HONEY: Later, I don't have time now!

EUGENE: I'll try to see that you never get hungry. I have a goose, and I have a dog!

HONEY: And underneath the canvas?

EUGENE: I don't know, that's a secret. People say there's a monument underneath and that it's covered up so that no one would be reminded of the past.

HONEY: All right, then, be careful.

EUGENE: Of what?

GERTIE: Deformation. Because, even though I invented you, sometimes fabrications get away, and, like tattered clouds in a strong wind, begin to change into the weirdest shapes!

EUGENE: That means, there's no pleasure without leisure!

HONEY: Later, I don't have time now! *(Exists.)*

EUGENE: But when you do have time, Mother, just you wait! Then it'll be me who won't have any! You're kidding yourself: my love isn't blind! Fetch!

ADAGIO: *(Enters):* Arf-arf-arf-arf-arf!
EUGENE: Goosie-goosie!
GERTIE: *(Enters):* Ga-ga-ga-ga-ga!
EUGENE: Are you dying of thirst?
THE SEVEN MAIDS *(Enter from all sides, excitedly, in song and dance):*

> Legs run around,
> Feet beat the ground.
> Behinds shake about,
> And bellies stick out.
> All souls quake,
> Backbones break!
> There's no need!
> Pffft!

(They falter.) Waaater! Waaaater! *(Exit.)*

EUGENE: What do you mean, "Water!" you son of a bitch?
ADAGIO: It wasn't me who asked for it!
THE SEVEN MAIDS *(Offstage):* Waaaaaater!
GERTIE: That's our parched, cracked mother earth crying for it.
EUGENE: I asked you: are you dying of thirst for revenge?
ADAGIO: Arf-arf-arf-arf!
GERTIE: Ga-ga-ga-ga-ga!
EUGENE: Stop yelping into the wind! Your teeth will fall out, and you won't have anything to bite with!
ADAGIO: I'm dying of thirst for knowledge...Arf-arf!
GERTIE AND ADAGIO *(In one voice):* Why! Why! Why does man live? Grrrr! Sssss!
EUGENE: That sounds more like death agony and wheezing than rebel cries!
ADAGIO: Yeah, mind you don't sneeze too hard; you might give up your ghost...Arf-arf!
GERTIE: I can't hold it any longer! *(Exits.)* Ga-ga-ga-ga-ga!
MACABRE *(Enters):* What are you doing here? (EUGENE *and* ADAGIO *sit up and beg like dogs.)*
EUGENE: Nothing in particular, Right Reverend. We're sitting on our haunches before you.

MACABRE: It's all right for him to beg; he's a dog.

ADAGIO: Arf-arf!

MACABRE But what are you doing with him?

EUGENE: That's what I'd like to know myself!

MACABRE All right, dismissed! *(They run wild.)* But that doesn't mean that now you should run and piss on me!

EUGENE: Fetch! *(They calm down.)*

MACABRE: Now what are you doing?

EUGENE: We're spreading ourselves out....

MACABRE: I appreciate your kindness, but with one small reservation. Namely, a big, wise father-regime must be very careful about whom he marries his beautiful, rich careers to. *(Kicks them.)* Scat! Shoo!

EUGENE *(To* Adagio*):* Get out of my way! Fetch! His Reverence is not in the mood for any nonsense! Out! *(*Adagio *goes off.)*

MACABRE *(To* Eugene*):* And you stay to listen!

EUGENE: I hope it'll be worth it?

MACABRE: I'll give you a shako. *(Gives him a shako.)*

EUGENE: Unh-unh. Would an ox head be too little for a cat to eat?

MACABRE: I'll give you a sash. *(Gives him a sash.)*

EUGENE: I'd do it for a lot less, to tell the truth. Why are you so generous?

MACABRE: I'm old and worn out.

EUGENE: You're never too old to kick!

MACABRE: There's no future for me, while the past is all mine—including our unforgettable love.

EUGENE: Maybe so, but you can't really see it.

MACABRE: Time conceals the truth, but I'll uncover it.

EUGENE: And what shall I do?

MACABRE Why, you'll chew on the canvas!

EUGENE: Until we chew memories down to the bone?

MACABRE: You'll find out in due course. Now go!

EUGENE: Where?

MACABRE: Upwards. Now you're a nobody, but when you get up with a sash around your shoulders and the shako around your ears, you'll be somebody! All doors will open before you because of the amulet you took with you, and, thus, you'll become somebody! *(*EUGENE *starts to leave.)*

GERTIE AND ADAGIO *(Enter):* Don't forget us! Ga-ga! Arf-arf! *(*EUGENE, GERTIE, ADAGIO, *and* MACABRE *exit.)*

THE SEVEN MAIDS *(Enter and in a frenzy):* Who's to keep us? Who's to feed us? When you're gone, who's to beat us?

HONEY *(Enters):* You wanted to bypass me, but you didn't know that the round robin goes clockwise! *(After her comes* EUGENE *dressed as a convict.)* And for that reason you've now been severely punished! Just as all doors opened before you when you kept your shako and sash as amulets, so now iron doors will slam shut behind you! *(Thunder.* HONEY *goes off.)*

EUGENE *(*GERTIE *and* ADAGIO *enter):* It's me, my goosie! My doggie! *(They exit.)* Your Eugene! *(*MACABRE *enters with* HONEY *who helps him along.)* Don't forget me! Tell my mother what's happened to me! *(Exits.)*

MACABRE: Cunty-Honey, why is it that there's always somebody here reminding somebody else to remember? And then they try not to forget?

HONEY: They're forever going up and down, up and down, and you can't make out anymore where the circle's head or tail is.

MACABRE: Let's stop then.

HONEY: Don't try! Your brakes are bad.

MACABRE: You're right, Honey, because everything in me is worn out and weak, just as you keep saying. I want to get stronger! *(Enter* EUGENE *dressed as a convict;* ADAGIO, *no longer a dog;* GERTIE, *no longer a goose; and* THE SEVEN MAIDS.*)*

THE SEVEN MAIDS *(Confusion):*

> I'm a seamstress,
> I sew up backs!
> My man's plain black!
> He lays down tracks!

ADAGIO: Visitors are coming: get the footstool ready for lunch!

THE SEVEN MAIDS *(Confusion):*

> I'm a beautician,
> And hair's my curse!
> My man's got a mission—
> He males each nurse!

MACABRE: Right you are, my dear children; your words are gold!

HONEY: No, Macabre! Don't do anything you haven't consulted me about beforehand! Don't be a mean old man! *(*MACABRE *snatches off the covering from the monument. All present are astonished and frightened.)*

ARTIE *(Stands like a statue—his own monument):* First of all, don't run away just because I've begun to speak! Naturally, I know the human heart rather well from before!

MACABRE: Vanity is the only thing that fills them with fear.

ALL: And poverty! And poverty!

ARTIE: Never fear, I won't demand a feast in memoriam! But if you just happen to have a boiled egg or chicken drumstick on you.

GERTIE: I have an egg, Macabre, the one you told me to bake on charcoal, as a cure for egg-sucking!

MACABRE: It's the same thing; peel it and feed him. *(She peels the egg and feeds* ARTIE.*)*

ARTIE: *(With his mouth full):* It's true that I'm made of iron, all hard and everlasting, but that doesn't mean much. Even cotton is sometimes harder than bone...and poverty is the hardest thing of all. Nevertheless! You should see the lonely head of a man on a pillow in a darkened room.

MACABRE: With twitching lips!

HONEY: And words that drip like venom!

ARTIE: No, that's no longer a talk; that's a conversation. And those aren't words like words in the light and the ears of others!

ALL: What is it? What is it?

ARTIE: That's more like sniffing around your own life...like a dog sniffing around a rubbish heap, where, if he's lucky, he may find a bone....

MACABRE: And a stone!

ARTIE: In their dreams and delirium, many cry over the grave of their homeland; but what really goes on in this world when we're awake?

MACABRE: Don't we see it, even though we look?

HONEY: Don't we hear it, even though we listen?

ADAGIO: Don't we spit it out, even though it disgusts us?

ARTIE: You, who sit at home, at conferences, and in offices!

MACABRE: Everything is done in the proper manner: by telephone interventions, official acts, diplomatic channels!

ARTIE: You're all wrong! *(All except* MACABRE *slowly go off.* MACABRE *and* ARTIE *from now on act as if in a dream.)* I'm always outside and I see when something rustles in the weeds, at the bottom...slowly seethes, like lava!...and overflows! It boils, and not one of you notices it! But on my pedestal the footsteps of history reverberate like gun salvoes! Thunderbolts shall still rip asunder these morasses of hot air. And all the illusions that you have woven over your heads shall scatter like scum!

MACABRE: Oh, my past! I may have made mistakes. Maybe I haven't done all that should have been done! Oh, my past. Maybe I went astray! Maybe I parted company with myself, and what I wanted to do went one way, while what I was able to do went the other way. Tell me!

ARTIE: No, it doesn't matter whether the hatter can play the bagpipes; people want to know what kind of headgear he's able to cut out for them! And when they hear that he's good and that he's made a lot of people happy, they all rush to him!

MACABRE: Oh, my past! Did I neglect you, poor dear, for the sake of others? Did I like them better than I did you, who have always been behind me, faithful as a shadow, with one end attached to my feet? Tell me!

ARTIE: Well, the master-hatter who's made caps for many people, pretty ones and expensive ones and thinking ones—he usually goes around wearing his own work-cap...because, if someone knows how to make a hood for a wise man, it doesn't mean that he himself can become a wise man by putting on a thinking cap! You must remember one thing: that whoever doesn't get what's his own might as well not have had anything at all!

MACABRE: Oh, my past, I'm not tired of you! And when I look at myself in you as in a mirror, I seem to be as young as a lily. Oh, my past, you give me strength, and I'm indebted to you for the entire future! *(*MACABRE *slowly sinks and falls asleep by the statue.)*

ARTIE: Don't touch what's not yours; take what belongs to you; otherwise it won't be acknowledged as such. And lives, those wasted as well as those fulfilled, will fill history, just as small drops of water fill a big river.

HONEY: *(Enters with* GERTIE*):* Shhh...Tippytoe...Let him get fast asleep before we fulfill his last wish. You know what his favorite dish is?

GERTIE: Stew of lies.

HONEY: But not like last time; it didn't turn out very well.

GERTIE: I oversalted it, but you know how he is: his mouth is always watering for that dish. He likes it whether it's got too much salt or too little.

ADAGIO *(Enters):* Goose!

GERTIE: Mongrel!

HONEY: All right, Adagio, didn't we say that we wouldn't mention the past anymore?

ADAGIO: But the statue is a permanent reminder.

HONEY: We'll turn it inside out like a glove!...that dark past, never fear! *(*MACABRE *wakes up.)* Quiet!

MACABRE: Has it gotten dark again?

HONEY, GERTIE, AND ADAGIO *(All together):* It has.

MACABRE: Hasn't the sun come up?

HONEY, GERTIE, AND ADAGIO *(All together):* It has.

MACABRE: Is it raining?

HONEY, GERTIE, AND ADAGIO *(All together):* It's pouring.

MACABRE: But I thought the sun was shining?

HONEY, GERTIE, AND ADAGIO *(All together):* It's broiling.

MACABRE: How do I look this morning?

HONEY, GERTIE, AND ADAGIO *(All together):* Fresh.

MACABRE: Oh, my past! Am I still able to make judgments when people are lying to me? Tell me, am I wise?

ADAGIO: Your mind warms up as light warms a man lost in darkness!

MACABRE: Oh, my past! I've destroyed you because of thgose who have never loved me. Tell me, am I popular?

HONEY: Your heart is like a lamb, meek and mild, and your soul is like a love bird during mating season; wherever you appear things come alive. Even the rocks start pulsating and breathing joy!

MACABRE: For years you poisoned me with the futility of stale water, and that corroded me like rust. Tell me, hasn't my strength been sapped?

GERTIE: Wherever you appear, even today, the earth opens up

under your feet! And where you point your finger, the mountains are rent asunder!

MACABRE *(Metamorphosis. Becomes erect, strong, and vigorous):* You lying sycophant. I've never been able to find out from you what's day and what's night! You lie to me because you hate me, and you hate me because you're afraid of me! And you wanted to poison me with lies! And you did poison me, but I've gotten over it. Look! *(Presses finger on the castle. The walls fall apart, something crashes. Thunder and lightning.)* I'm still powerful! Hats off! *(More thunder, all are petrified.)*

EUGENE: Please, Eugene here....

MACABRE: You've come, just at the right time!

EUGENE: No, I can come later. I'm used to being put off.

HONEY *(Pushes* EUGENE *forward):* Now! Now! Now or never!

MACABRE: You've been wanting a chance to say something for ages, so there you are. You're finally free to say what's on your mind!

EUGENE *(More to himself):* For so many years now this has been my winning card. Must I really get into a mess so near the end?

MACABRE: Don't mumble; quickly say what you have to say!

EUGENE: I don't have anything to say.

MACABRE: What, then?

EUGENE: I've been leading everyone up the garden path for years now. I've been living on my own mysteriousness. I'm a figment of the imagination.

MACABRE: You wretch, off with your hat, too!

EUGENE: But I don't own a hat.

HONEY: So much the worse for you! Instead of your hat, it'll be off with your head! Hit him! Let him be the scapegoat! *(Confusion. Scuffling. Crowding, they close the circle around* EUGENE.*)*

COLLECTIVE SPEECH

MACABRE: The only truth for me is my path and those who go along this way, to the hills far way!

ADAGIO: If I'm ever again a regime son-in-law, I'll know how to arrange my cherished career!

HONEY: Give me a salt pestle!

ARTIE: And the past is as true as it is false!

GERTIE: And they'll choke me again like a goose, in bed—that's for sure!

MACABRE: Oh, my past, I'm never tired of you! *(Separates himself from the crowd and sits on the throne.)*

ARTIE: Don't touch other people's property. Just take what belongs to you, or else you won't get any credit for it.

(The end of the collective speech. The crowd opens up and EUGENE *comes out of the circle, again as a general with an officer's cap and sash.)*

HONEY *(To* EUGENE*):* Come on now, report!

EUGENE *(Goes before* MACABRE *on the throne):* All the wolves are satisfied, Right Reverend, and no goats are missing!

MACABRE AND THE REST *(Rises from the throne and goes to the footlights, followed by all the others. In one voice):* And thus, we've finished our walk through history. . . . *(The lights dim.)*

THE END

Translated by E.J. Czerwinski

ŽARKO PETAN

(b. 1929)

Petan was born in Ljubljana, Slovenia. He is known primarily as a satirical and dramatic writer. Currently, Petan is employed at the Academy of Motion Pictures and Television. His works, which have been translated into numerous languages, include: *Parents for Sale* (1964), *One Word Does Not Bother* (1964), and *Forbidden Slogans* (1966).

Petan, the author of many humorous and satirical poems, is a typical representative of the young Slovenian generation. Especially popular are his aphorisms, some of which have an enduring value, reflecting the changing attitudes in Slovenia in strongly ironic overtones.

Aphorisms

He who asks will be asked.

Man is a renter of his own skin.

I don't understand why prices are running wild only upward.

Psychoanalysis is a journey around oneself.

It is, unfortunately, impossible to inherit life experience.

The greatest art is to keep silent talkatively.

The latest technical achievement: a flat-iron for the brain.

A question mark is a pick which has become curious.

The world has changed so much it does not recognize me any more.

Politics do not change the world, they only paint it over and over.

Terrorists are suicides who prefer to die in a group.

Justice has its eyes covered, injustice its mouth.

Low blows land best from high positions.

Very often it is best when you bury your deep thoughts as deep as you can.

A loud lie can be heard in the ninth village.

Translated by Vasa D. Mihailovich

VLADA BULATOVIĆ-VIB
(b. 1931)

Born in Sopotsko, Macedonia, Bulatović—along with Crnčević and Bećković—is one of the most prominent names of modern Serbian satire. Writing in the tradition of Domanović and Nušić, Bulatović showed his great talent in his book *Alarm Clock* (1963). Since his satire is concise and easy to read, his popularity is widespread.

As the following stories indicate, Bulatović had a fine ear for the contemporary vernacular and an ability to create satire without excessive distortion. His satire reveals his "social message" through a series of self-incriminating monologues and dialogues, revealing all the tragicomedy, innuendoes, and associations.

The Illness

THE CONGRESS OF MEDICAL WORKERS was greeted in the name of their patients by a man whose palms had grown together. The invalid looked like a believer praying or like someone who had been clapping for a long time in frost.

The story of his illness was extremely interesting. There were two tired doctors in the first row who actually talked about him; they were not listening to the report, as they had been the day before at the Congress of Traumatologists.

"That's my patient. He came one day with joined hands. He shoved his hand into my face and shouted: 'Hear! Hear!' and 'Long live.' " I tried to take his case history.

"What is your name?" I asked him.

"Hear! Hear!" he replied.

"Occupation?" I asked.

"Long live!" he shouted.

I had to anesthetize him before I could talk to him.

"What's your occupation?" I asked him when he was unconscious.

"Attendant."

"What kind of attendant? State your specialization."

"Attendant at the congress hall."

"How long have you been employed?"

150

"A year now."

"How did your hands come to grow together?"

"I started working the congress hall just when there was a Congress of Cynologists on. Someone was reading a report. It was all about the fact that man must love dogs. One comrade was reading the report and the others kept interrupting him and shouting, 'Hear! Hear!' and 'Long live.' Why don't you applaud?"

"I'm not at the congress. I work here. I'm a servant here."

"It doesn't matter," he said. "Shout and applaud. There are newspapermen here. If they notice that just one person is not applauding they will write, 'The conclusions were not received unanimously.' " And so I, too, started to shout and to beat one palm against the other.

"Then, in the fall, there were congresses of foraminifers, collectors of subscriptions, activists, and pensioners, madrigalists and contrabassists, telephonists and telecontrollers, town peasants and village brides, voluntary givers of membership-fees, margarine producers, ecologists, godologists, biologists, bontonogists, minalonologists, beneologists, well-makers, goldsmiths, journalists, cowkeepers, doctors, cheesemakers, paranoids. . . .

"They changed everyday, but I stayed and I shouted, 'Hear! Hear!' and 'Long live!' with them all and beat my hands together.

"Ten days ago at a Congress of Siamese Twins, during the report, I tried to applaud, my palms moved towards each other and stayed that way."

The next day at the Congress of Semi-invalids, the man with joined palms, was proposed as minutes keeper.

The proposition was accepted unanimously.

Translated by Nada Ćurićija-Prodanović

The Shark and
The Bureaucrat

ONE DAY, FISHING ON THE SEASHORE, the Bureaucrat saw the Shark. He said to it:

"I marvel at you, Shark!"

"And I marvel at you, Bureaucrat!"

"You swim wonderfully."

"So do you."

"You are strong, Shark."

"It is nothing compared to your strength."

"I wanted to ask you: How do you manage to keep going in so much water?"

"Quite simply. When it gets cold, I go under; when it gets warm, I come up. That's why I swim only in my own circle."

"You are a big fish, but now it's no longer fashionable to say: 'Big fish eat little ones.' How do you feed yourself under the new conditions?"

"I fight for equality. For example, I say to the whitebait: 'Do you want us to be equal?' 'Yes,' it says. 'Then, go ahead, swallow me,' I say. It tries and can't. Then I try and can."

"How do you teach the whitebait to obey?"

"I take up a pedagogical position."

"What did you say: demagogical?"

"I said: pedagogical. I say to the whitebait: 'You ought to be

ashamed of yourselves. How can you swim in different directions?'
They are ashamed and swim in my direction. I open my mouth to
greet them with enthusiastic welcome, but they are impulsive and
rush to my throat by mistake.''

"When people start to criticize you, Shark, what do you do?''

"I turn over onto my back and swim lazily like a corpse. Then I
allow the whitebait to spread me and nibble at me.''

"How does a shark make a career?''

"I don't understand.''

"For example, first you are a shark in one town, then in a larger
field, in a district; then you swim further and further.''

"We don't have any of that. The sea is not divided, and climbing
upwards is limited. You can only go as far as the surface.''

"I shouldn't want much more. I, too, would like to swim up to
the surface.''

"Just be a bit more cunning. When whales notice your tendency
to swim to the surface, you admit that your tail smells and renounce it. And don't worry, a new and better tail will grow.''

"What is your position, Shark?''

"Normal. Head down, tail up, fins at the side.''

"I don't mean that. I was thinking of your function.''

"Oh, that. With us the fish that swims fastest succeeds.''

"You lucky fish.''

The Shark proffered its fins as a sign of parting. The Bureaucrat
in shaking hands, leaned too far forward and fell into the sea.
Some time later, the Bureaucrat came out of the water with the
Shark in his teeth.

Translated by Nada Ćurćija-Prodanović

The Municipal Whale

In the little town of Smalton there was a little Town Hall, a little school, a little house of little culture, a rivulet. One day a large consignment arrived in Smalton. Petar, the emigrant from Smalton, had sent a live whale! Let his hometown see that he had gotten somewhere in the outside world.

The delighted mayor of Smalton, in the rivulet, in water up to his waist, waited for the whale with a bouquet of flowers. The ceremony was a success although the mayor hardly managed to get out of the overflowing river.

The rivulet dried up. The whale laughed at those present. The citizens were requested to leave their work and to use all available means to bring back the water.

A notice was put up on the shore:

Municipal Whale. Under State Protection. Citizens are requested not to swear as the animal is very sensitive.

Two days later the whale grew pale.

In the presence of the mayor it was examined by the town veterinarian who said: "This water is too fresh for it. And besides, music disturbs it."

The next day an order was issued for the municipal workers to salt the river from seven to nine.

Music was banned from the town.

Firemen kept guard beside the whale.

Three days later the whale turned green.

Work in the new salt works, instituted only for the whale, was brought to a halt.

The veterinarian remembered that the whale was a mammal.

A dairy was established. They salted the milk and gave it to the whale in a bottle.

The whale turned yellow.

They dismissed the veterinarian.

The teat factory stopped work.

Then the mayor took his wife's advice. They fed the whale cake. The whale turned red.

The mayor relied on his own common sense: the whale needed the sea.

He went to the capital with the electorate. He went to find money to carry out the greatest project of his commune—that of the municipal whale.

According to the electorate, the Adriatic Sea had to be poured into the Smalton rivulet.

They got the money.

It all went to founding the Institute for Research into the Whale on Land.

The municipal sea-water contribution was brought into practice.

Citizens were cautioned to economize on water.

Apart from that, they were requested not to make a noise during the day—the whale usually slept then.

The mayor was preparing to go for new investments when a fireman ran up to inform him that the whale was not moving.

Then the three of them burst into tears.

The rivulet swelled from the tears. The whale began to move; it liked the salt water.

From that day on, the townsfold poured tears uninterruptedly into the rivulet.

The whale is doing fine.

Translated by Nada Ćurćija-Prodanović

Lavoratore and Bureaucratsia

COMRADE LAVORATORE SUPPORTED himself with his ten fingers. In the morning he worked for a decadent bourgeois, in the afternoon he whistled the Internationale. He spent his nights in his landlord's cellar.

Everything became unbearable. His existence and this position. But most of all the bourgeois' daughter, Miss Anna Maria Bureaucratsia. She put paragraphs under his pillow and brought out his soul for inspection. She rode him piggyback. She climbed onto his head and thought up horrors.

Lavoratore dreamed terrible dreams at night. That he was putting Miss Anna Maria Bureaucratsia between the covers of Marx's *Das Kapital* and climbing onto the cover. The young lady expired. From the wall, in his frame, Engels applauded.

From dreams, the proletarian Lavoratore turned to reality. He became overripe and began to set up a new order of things. He chased Daddy Bourgeois into the cellar. He chucked Daddy's little daughter, Anna Maria Bureaucratsia, over his shoulder.

Bruised from the fall and fear, Anna Maria Bureaucratsia hid in the cellar with her daddy. There she grew pale and prettier.

When Lavoratore got over his fury, Anna waited for him at the gate and looked at little dogs.

One day, Comrade Lavoratore would pour a bowl of dirty water

156

over Miss Anna Maria Bureaucratsia from the balcony. She would whimper joyfully, clap her hands and shout: "I want more! Wet me!"

At night, of her own accord, she took Lavoratore's socks and washed them in secret. Once she happened to cross the courtyard in her petticoat. Afterwards she came to confess that she had consciously undressed but only in front of him and only for him. Once she called him at night when she was quite naked and fell into his lap. He was disgusted but felt warm. She sent him love letters in verse and prose: "You will not escape me, I can tell you, my darling. I want your just worker's arms to squeeze me and smother me."

Lavoratore squeezed her with his just arms but did not smother her. He could not; he saw devotion in her eyes.

He took her to work in his house.

Anna Maria Bureaucratsia made his bed ready and herself in it.

Comrade Lavoratore betrayed personal weakness. Anna, personal strength.

In truth, he did scold her in public: "She will suffocate me like before. I shall chase her away. I'll burn her, I'll crush her!"

At home Anna Maria Bureaucratsia would wait for him. She would wait for Lavoratore to come home and hum. When he arrived she would ride him piggy-back out of tenderness.

Comrade Lavoratore would bend down a little, out of tenderness, of course. Anna Maria Bureaucratsia got round, plump, and full. It was a squeeze in bed because of her. Lavoratore had bad dreams. Anna Maria Bureaucratsia was putting him between book covers and squashing him from above and below.

He awoke from his bad dreams ready to chase her away. But he glanced at her. Who would chase away such a gorgeous woman?

What do you say, Citizen, is it time to tell the man to interfere in his love affairs?

If it is time, let us hurry! For Lavoratore's little companion, Anna Maria Bureaucratsia, might get pregnant.

Translated by Nada Ćurćija-Prodanović

The Ugly Duckling

A DUCK WAS SITTING on her eggs and waiting for them to hatch.

They hatched wonderful even-yellow ducklings, and one square, ugly, distorted duckling.

The birds mocked at the ugly duckling; the mother duck became white with sorrow and shed tears. The birds continued to make fun: "Some ducks cry at their ugly small fry."

It was the same, day after day. For instance, the duck would take her little ones for a walk. The even-yellow duck waddled proudly; the square one did not know how: it rolled.

Finally, one day, the ducklings waddled out into the world.

The first duckling wrote reports and always received pay.

The second duckling read reports and was regularly paid.

The third duckling extracted quotations and received monthly pay.

The fourth patched up plans and got his pay.

The ugly duckling could not leave the house because of the laughter. He sat at home and pecked at words. When it had pecked up learning, the ugly duckling thought up revenge and set out into education.

Once again the birds cackled and quacked: "Duckie's sad, its life is bad."

The square duckling put his glasses on his nose every

morning, and, with his notebook under his wing, he went to the duck's school. Sometimes he would get something in the way of pay for some little something to cover his ugliness. They neither asked whether he ate nor did he eat.

What would an ugly duckling do with food when he is full of learning?

In the evening, when the duckling returned from school, the birds mocked at him: "You and your learning—good luck! You're still just an ugly duck."

In his whole life the square duckling could not get any lower. He decided to climb high. He got up on a bench and hanged himself from the school bell.

When the doctors examined him, they found out that the ugly duckling was a swan.

The next day the papers, in the obituaries, chided the ugly duckling for being impatient: why hadn't he waited until the other birds saw that he was a swan?

Translated by Nada Ćurćija-Prodanović

BORA ĆOSIĆ
(b. 1932)

Ćosić was born in Zagreb. He has been living in Belgrade since 1937 and has written both poetry and prose. Associated with a number of literary journals, he is best known as editor of *Literary Gazette*, a prominent Belgrade literary paper. Ćosić is primarily a prose writer, who has recently turned to satire. Some of his works are: *House of Thieves* (1956), *The Angel Came for His Own* (1959), *Tales of the Trades* (1962), and *The Role of My Family in the World Revolution* (1969).

Ćosić is familiar to Yugoslav audiences for his unique literary approach; in most cases, his plot consists of short perceptive comments spoken by characters on such common subjects as historical events and heroes, social change, or life in general. Thus, the body of his work is fragmentary; the style, telegraphic and pithy. Most of his humor and satire is light, even when touching the serious. Occasionally, this light satire becomes cynical, as in his story "The King of the Poets."

The King of the Poets

WHEN BRAG THE GREAT NATIONAL POET came to our town—at that
time he was quite unknown—he went into the writers' café to look
for the king of the poets or someone acting on his behalf.

"What do you want with the king?" they asked him. "Perhaps
we have a king and perhaps we haven't."

Brag looked grim and gloomy. He had no wish to discuss the
matter with just any ordinary poet.

"I want the king," he said at last. "It's just that I want to knock
his teeth out."

The poets smiled slyly to themselves. Brag grabbed hold of the
one nearest at hand and gave him a resounding thump to the credit
account of a king who did not even exist. The man he clobbered
slumped beneath the table, and the newly arrived poet asked his
friends for something to eat. They gave him sausages, wine, and
their poems.

"I am the greatest poet in Serbia," Brag proclaimed, "and, for
this reason, I permit you to offer me food."

The poets began to talk about this, the greatest of them all. Brag
caught hold of women in the street by their breasts, got himself
beaten up, and arrested. He embarked upon an amorous pursuit of
Rosy, a one-legged tart from the railway station, or Anny, the
decrepit cashier from Kate's café, or fat village wenches who

161

brought cabbages to the vegetable market. He was hopelessly in love with Greta, the cook in the Commercial Hotel; he drooled beneath the window of the lavatory attendant on Republic Square; he flung himself under the legs of a toothless conductress on Bus 34. He loved women utterly, devotedly, ceaselessly. He wrote poems about being and about nothingness, about puerility and about death.

His poems were as incomprehensible to the shop assistants he slept with as to the poets who fed him. They appeared in every magazine. He was the greatest national poet of the first years following the war. Then his great performance began.

He burst through café doors, fraternized with tramps, jumped head first from the lower stories. He was beaten up by drunks on the docks, by policemen, by the husbands of receptionists, and even, at length, by the poets themselves, who were becoming frightened by his fantastic fame. His poems were turbid and well-fashioned. They gave an incredible picture of love, revolution, and life in general. Brag became more and more popular and began to appear in school textbooks; the children read him with fear and sweat on their brows. He used to sleep with the gypsies under the bridge over the Sava.

At a large poetry meeting, Brag, as the first great national poet after so many years of silence, bawled out in his drunken voice the most beautiful things about the Republic ever written. The Republic honored its son and applauded. The poet went about without socks because of the heat. His poems were powerfully passionate, melodic, and frightening. His toothless mistress, the old women he chased, the little, flat-chested waitress, all listened to his brilliant, drunken recitals with closed eyes, without understanding. The great national poet, Brag, crossed Republic Square in the middle of the day on his knees in homage to the lavatory attendant there. Below, in the stench of disinfectant in the Ladies' Room—ignoring all rules of decorum—he composed four sonnets on the future, the most beautiful of their kind, while kneeling among the lavatory brushes. The girls of the entire city—young undergraduates, lesbians, activists, daughters of respectable families—were crazy about his poems and not a little about him.

At the evening literary gatherings in the parks or in faculty halls or by the pedestals of huge statues, they would ask him in tremulous tones how he succeeded in writing so warmly, so rapturously, so fabulously, above all, so well. He smiled in his innocent way beneath his heavy spectacle frames, showed his small teeth awry, and explained that he did it to infuriate the others. The virgins were amazed at the simplicity of the poet's reply, and he, instead of doing anything else, read another six scintillating sonnets about Eve, his newly acquired mistress.

The poets, eaten away by despair and jealousy, gave up feeding him. Their published verses did not bring in enough even to pay for his drinks. And the national poet, forgetting his pride, knocked on the doors of various national bodies looking for something to eat. They led the king of the poets, ravenous as he was, into their reception rooms, entertained him handsomely, and introduced him to various foreign literary figures who were friends of the Republic. Brag devoured fine cuts of meat and swore at the mother of the host in French. Then he stood up and recited his translations of Valery, which were excellent. At night, he returned to the windows of the hospitable house, and, drunk and cold, poured out great curses on humanity, on the French, and on any and everything else.

Learning of Brag's, fame through the newspapers, his relations began to arrive from the village: brothers with cudgels, brothers-in-law, and finally his father himself.

They took over their forgotten Brag, now that he was a great and highly esteemed poet. His brother went to the editors haggling for each verse; the father threatened the publishers with an ominous stick he himself had carved. The books came out on time, beautifully bound. The brothers, with their bloodshot eyes, went into fine shops to buy their brother the most expensive socks. The brothers-in-law chased away the poet's mistress, the hunchbacked street-walkers full of sensitivity, the one-eyed tram drivers, and others. Life to the great poet became desolate, and, because of this, he set out on foot along the road to the south. He went along wide roads, nibbling coarse grass, puffing at dandelion seeds, and gazing at the clouds high over the flat country. After three days he reached the frontier near Subotica.

"Where are you going to?" the border people asked gaily.

"To Budapest," Brag replied. "I am a poet and a better one than anyone else. I want to see what the Danube at Budapest is like and write a poem about it."

Expressing their regret, they informed him that, without a passport, he could not go to Budapest, nor indeed, to any place abroad. He looked at them politely and asked when it would be possible to go to Budapest and to all those other wonderful places in the world without a passport. They replied that they did not know, but that, at present, it was not possible. So the poet Brag returned from the frontier of the Republic, whistling, nibbling grass, happy, but a little tired.

On the way he held poetry meetings in the villages, factories, and football stadiums. The people flocked and, standing, listened solemnly to his endless recitations.

His brothers in their house on the outskirts sorted out the poet's papers, stuck his photographs which had appeared in fashion magazines on the walls, and weeded the grass around the house. They even bought a radio. The poet fled from his fine relations, wrote dark and brilliant sonnets on great metaphysical problems, on human blood, on diaphragms, and other organs, on chimeras, wars and such things, and on life. Only once did he take a fancy to a fair girl; a graceful secondary-school girl, the granddaughter of P. Bosustov, a social confessor. She tried to take him with her fragile, manicured fingers. For six days he wore shirts whiter than white; for six days he sported expensive ties and drank only mineral water. He discussed poetry only in the sublime manner; he listened to classical music, subtle and unceasing; he lived in another great and polished world. That woman lulled him thither with her breasts, her eyes, and her arms, but on the seventh day, according to Biblical finality, he got disgustingly drunk, ate onions, took off his socks which he found too warm. Bosustov's granddaughter asked him if this meant that something had happened to them, and he replied with an alcoholic blandness that what had happened was that he could no longer stand such a fine but hellish life.

Finding himself once more in the street, the great national poet felt an explicable coldness in his heart: a loneliness hard as stone gripped the poet's soul. He went into a telephone booth, that station of human understanding, but was unable to find a friendly number; so he called up the world, mankind: "Oh, world"—he cried—"where are you?" But the world, that great community without loneliness and warmth, did not reply.

In the cafés sat circus dog trainers, acrobats, gamblers, menders of broken plates, as well as very young poets.

In the pungent smelling cafés, propped up against the counter, stood many citizens of the new age, talented short story writers, impeded by alcohol, do-gooders, and lunatics, some of who recited *sotto voce* with poignancy and enchantment. Their poems turned on the wheels of history, on aspects of the female form, on everything. The poets were young, unschooled in the matters of life and did not know where to turn with their painful and blasphemous poetry.

These noble minds, distracted by history, once more adopted the king of the poets, Brag, as their comrade. He was no longer alone, and great festivals of poetry-reading began to take place. The audiences were moved to the brink of tears.

Brag once more took heart and explained at last the great significance of his art—the witness of a new age. Brag became possessed and fired with a new zeal. He addressed the philosophers, cataleptics, idiosyncratics of the whole world. He explained that, by means of special electrodes, he controlled the growth of plants. He convinced them over and over again, that the threads of many important events, even those relating to traffic and contraception, passed through his pulsating brain. Clutching his breast in pain, he confessed what an effort it was for him to renew by his own forces the daylight of every morning at precisely the appointed time. He had no fear of competition from the fearful lady versifiers nor from the vulgar poetasters who gathered around. The poet explained the formula of his inconceivable verse. A great force was in the king of the poets when he spoke.

And then, in the middle of an enormous celebration of great words, the lavatory attendant, accompanied by her three-year-old son, hobbled in on a large crutch. The poets looked at the newcomer in a drunken way; the dog trainers, insulted, began to leave the table. They asked her what she was doing at such a function: the greatest poetry festival since the war. She said that she had more claim on the great poet than any one of them because she had given him a son, the three-year-old urchin she had brought with her. The poets began to swear and curse, calling her a lying whore; the king looked at the child without any sign of recollection. The sweet young things (the sort to be found in a café) wanted to approach the child who, although dirty, looked very sweet, but the frightful lavatory attendant, mother of the poet's offspring, said outrageous things and, dangerously brandishing her crutch, spat at them continuously.

And Brag, the king, denying his paternity, began to stroll from café to café followed by the versifiers, the possessors of great words, the masters of sincere verse, all very drunk. He showed them all what he could do with his enormous brain-force; many of them asked if he could do this, that, or the other, and the poet's answer was always that he could.

Then John of the Underground, the critic of life, the classicist of forbidden thought, the great respecter of self-imposed cruelty, stood up and, from his tattered pocket, drew a revolver captured from the occupation forces and asked a question about the death wish. Looking at the bloodshot eyes of the great poet, he of the underground, humbly and quietly asked if the king could answer this final challenge of history. Brag, without a flicker of expression, took the revolver from John, put the muzzle into his mouth and pulled the trigger.

To the cemetery flocked the poets, the revolutionary leaders, the citizens of our matchless city and its outskirts. At a discreet distance, behind the other tombstones defaced by the rain, stood the great loves of the national figure, those little old lame and syphilitic women.

You will find in P. Bosustov's study an imposing collection preserved in formalin. The collection includes an index finger, allegedly belonging to Brag and reputed to have been lost in a café brawl. For many years, poets, blinded by grief and drink, have been paying the unemployed social confessor a small income to kneel before the legendary formalin unicate which, in defiance of chemistry, is dissolving in the green chartreuse-like liquid. It is not really known, however, whether the great poet was buried without or—which is more probable—with all ten fingers. In favor of the latter conjecture we animadvert to the curt notice, inserted by the proletarian writer, D. Vidović, in all newspapers on the day of the death of this young leader: "STRANGE EVENT—HE HAD EVERYTHING!"

Translated by Harold Norminton

BRANA CRNČEVIĆ

(b. 1935)

Born in Ruma, Crnčević is known as one of the leading Serbian satirists and poets. In the early 70's, he was the editor of *Jež* (The Hedgehog), a very popular Belgrade humorous magazine. He has written TV plays and poems for children. He is best known for his book of aphorisms, *Speak as You Are Silent* (1963).

Crnčević is one of the most prominent representatives of intellectual satire, an outspoken form often characterized by well-aimed commentary on current issues.

Write as You Are Silent

Since I heard what I think, I don't believe what I hear.

A fool goes backward even with progressive ideas.

Unbelievable, I hear my opinion more often than I say it.

If a victim returned to the place of crime, the murderer would kill him again.

Life is that sand into which we sink the deepest.

What is the use of a new wave when the water is old.

Of all points, I am most interested in the one at which the victim becomes a murderer.

One says we, too, will dream of a better past.

No one can force me to think all I say.

To love means to destroy bridges before oneself.

In the search of truth there are too many lies.

Justice which only punishes becomes injustice.

It is always less tragic when a leader dies for the people than when the people die for a leader.

To kill an immortal is the dream of every good hangman.

Who thinks shallow will never drown.

There are cells in the brain and chambers in the heart; what a concentration camp in every head!

When a tyrant rises above the ground, he must first overcome the earth's gravity.

Do not rush so much into history; from history nobody returns alive.

The man at the bottom asks the man at the top to meet in the middle.

To Blacks it seems that Whites are equal.

Who does not like my life, let him live his own.

It is easy to be wrong; why don't you be right for once?

Who has not climbed anywhere has nowhere to fall from.

To die for means to live against.

The heart has friends, the brain is alone.

There were two comrades: one fell for the country, the other on the country.

When I want to stay awake I count the hunters.

Small nations suffer from generous understanding.

A revolution does not eat its own children, but the grownups better be cautious.

We are all dolls. When you press a man, he cries, "Mama!"

From the bottom everything is high; from the top everything is deep.

If it were not for the telephone, the obedient would not have a connection with the brain.

The impatient, too, want into the future by a shortcut.

Translated by Vasa D. Mihailovich

Prosperity

PEOPLE ARE PROVIDING evidence that prosperity is growing. I know that this is so, although I don't tolerate serious proof. I know that prosperity is growing; I can even see it from my angle.

How?

In this way:

Proof 1. In the window which was already full of lambs' meat, the butcher in my street put a sign saying, "We have animals."

Proof 2. A lot of girls are nicely dressed and sway their derrières while walking. The proof for this is the fact that they sway their derrières.

Proof 3. The increased number of pop songs. People who sing such studipities have no worries.

Proof 4. An increased number of divorces proves that a man who works at two jobs surely earns his money from the third.

Proof 5. There is a relatively large number of young people retiring. When it is so good for young retired people, how good it must be for the old ones.

Proof 6. The sentence, "You are a donkey," has been modified. A donkey is an animal which pulls exclusively for others.

Proof 7. I saw a woman with gloves who was driving a Buick. If you please, how did she get the gloves?

Proof 8. The cabinetmakers perform abortions on straight chairs and build plush lounging chairs. Each lounging chair has its master, and each is master of a lounger.

Proof 9. There are an alarming number of people spending their time in bars. For me, that is proof that they are spending their time.

Proof 10. There is a crisis in housing. All people want to have their own apartments. Such desires are on a steady increase. These increased desires are characteristic of prosperity.

Proof 11. There is a growing number of people saying, "I will show you!" as they brandish their fists.

Proof 12. There is an ever-increasing number of car accidents and a decreasing number involving pedestrians.

Because of superstition, of course, I did not look for the 13th proof.

This game of gathering proofs can be played endlessly, but under the condition that each participant gathers only one to twelve proofs.

Translated by Branko Mikasinovich

Aphorisms

The wakeful have awaited the dawn; now they are sleepy.

Man is a great thing!

I have collided with the blind man. It is my fault.

Thanks to justice, the corpse has won the suit.

Two and two makes four—whenever the circumstances allow it.

The fuller the jails the nearer the freedom.

He who writes in his own blood won't do it for too long.

Make us a list of ideas which we are allowed to arrive at.

You cannot reach the stars on foot.

Now we can freely say that there is no freedom of speech.

Leave me alone. I am a revolutionary!

When the torturers are clever, the cries are not heard.

The standard is rising—the people are getting smaller.

Life is like a masked ball: when everyone takes off his mask, the merriment stops.

People kill each other trying to prove that their system is more humane.

A politician is a man whom we pay well to tell us how well we live.

To lead someone—do you have to turn your back to him?

Historians should be thanked for many bright pages of our history.

A nightingale retains its beautiful voice even behind bars.

While hitting the head against the wall, the strongest fare the worst.

By crawling in war we used to get to our enemies. By crawling in peace we are reaching our friends.

The weakness of a ruler lies in the strength of his bodyguards.

The blind don't see that others have eyes.

The deeper you bow, the higher your rear end.

Truth and justice are so honest they seldom leave descendants behind.

A man with his back made of dough is never without bread.

Only in fear is everyone of the same opinion.

The persecution of intelligent men belongs to the cultural exchange between states.

Man is our greatest wealth, so say the merchants.

We are descendants of a monkey who cut the branch on which he sat.

Leaders of the proletarians of all countries—unite!

His head cost him his head.

Silence is bad for a society, but a blessing for an individual.

Translated by Vasa D. Mihailovich

ŽIVKO ČINGO

(b. 1935)

Čingo was born in the village of Velegošte near Ohrid, Macedonia. He has published two collections of short stories, *Pelasgian* (1963) and *New Pelasgian* (1965). He is one of the few Macedonians who has tried his writing skills at satire. Each of his stories is a vivid vignette of Macedonian peasant life in the years after 1945 when the Revolution and the new way of life came to the Macedonian villages. The new manner of existence, with its commissars, slogans, and mass meetings, appears in Čingo's short stories as a thin veneer on the old peasant way of life. New holidays are celebrated as if they were old pagan rites with people drinking heavily, heavy-breasted women longing for love, and nature in blossom. Čingo is able to permeate such scenes with color, smells, and often satirical shapes which are full of life.

At the time when many contemporary writers seek out morbid, psychological themes from urban life, it is refreshing to read Čingo and find oneself close to rural life, the earth, and the peasant wit.

The Medal

PASKVEL IS CERTAINLY the most beautiful village in our valley, but, to tell the truth, it's not the setting for a tale. It's so far away from the whole world. Even from the nearest highway, one must walk many kilometers in order to get to the village. But now it, too, no longer exists. Old man Noer Levkovski said, my dear cousin, that Paskvel has gone to the devil. Our Paskvel has died, my dear little child. Poor Paskvel! And it used to give birth to such falcons. Both men and women, as only the good Lord could desire. Those were real people. For example, our neighbors the Devijevs, Uncle Nazer, Uncle Laster Trajceski (may they rest in peace). Ah, what giants! And, if we want the truth, what a player Uncle From was. I bet you couldn't find such a marvelous bagpiper for miles around. Perhaps you will say, "So what! A player, and a bagpiper at that!" But it's not quite so. Let the good saints punish me if Uncle From weren't something like thunder. But, as it is, even Uncle From has left.

Everyone! Everyone has left Paskvel. Now surely the woods have grown up all around it. Perhaps the birds came down from the mountain and moved into the warm nests of the people. Perhaps even the Paskvelian vineyards have withered up. And a vine is like a person. Abandoned, it quickly dries up. The small vineyard sheds up on the hill have surely grown desolate. And directly below was the valley. All green, of course, in the spring. This is precisely what

176

I want to tell you about. It was spring then, and the whole valley was green. But maybe it was the end of spring, and the valley was not green. No, maybe it wasn't really all like that; but you must believe me that the leaves touched the sky and it trembled in greenness. All the surroundings, too, attained the golden green color of the sun and foliage. Perhaps, really, it wasn't all like that, you understand; but, the devil take me, it all looked that way to me. I was in love. Yes, a man fell in love, not worrying about time. And I was devilishly, foolishly in love. I was done for, my dear comrades. Ah, that was love!...a devilish love. I fell in love with the constable's daughter, Itrina Isailovska. Lightning struck us down, both me and her. What a time for that to happen!

No, it seemed then that time didn't exist at all. It was reduced to trysts. So it passed quickly—even that little moment stolen from the day. When we climbed to the vineyards, stealthily like rabbits because it was still dusk and everyone could see us, as soon as we sat down on the ground, there it was, the appointed hour. All around us the boys and girls called to each other, singing some new shock workers' song. My little brother whistled incessantly and called me with a trembling voice. Ah, that voice, that whistle! I almost began to hate my younger brother. His damned whistling and that voice of Itrina Isailovska. A man lived as if on fire.

"Are you coming, my little angel?" Itrina whispered in a soft, muffled voice.

Oh, that voice, my dear people; I don't remember another voice like it. It was something like the river glistening below in the valley, all liquid and afire from the evening sun. Such was the voice of my good Itrina.

"Are you coming?" she whispered. "Are you coming, my gentle foal?" Itrina spoke panting, lying in the green vines. Oh, people, people! And the warm earth, so warm it almost burned. From that flame, a man couldn't open his eyes to look around. Everything was topsy-turvy. Only that voice of Itrina, so clear and insistent.

"Why are you leaving, my dear?" she asked. "Am I not good, God strike me?"

"Let it be, Itrina," I muttered. "Let it be. Don't make it hard for me. You don't understand. I must go."

"My God!" she said and took white flowers from her lips, and with the other hand slowly unbuttoned her blouse. "Oh, my God!" she whispered. "I am such a slut. Argil Petronievski, I am a great curse. No one loves me. I am a devil. Everyone runs from me."

"No, no," I consoled her, bending over her high forehead, and, if a man bends over Itrina, he's a fool if he doesn't fall all the way. A man simply loses his head. He melts.

"Hey, Argil, the secretary is coming, Comrade Leunko!" floated the frightened voice of my younger brother. "Hurry, fool, hurry! The secretary's already here."

"Oh, that's all I need, the secretary," I thought, and large beads of sweat broke out over my entire body. Cold shivers ran through my veins. "Well, it's the secretary, Comrade Secretary," I recalled, and before my eyes appeared a mist and horrible images. Whatever a man thought, wherever he looked, Comrade Secretary was everywhere. Comrade Leunko with his bloated and unshaven face. And his nose straight and serious. That, however, wasn't important. His eyes were sunken and dark. Comrade Secretary certainly slept very little. That much must be admitted. A look sharp like a sabre. It would cut down everything before him. A look like a steel sword. And a voice so clear and loud. A merciless voice.

"Hm, let's examine ourselves, comrades. Let us give a report in sector one, five, eight, thirteen....Let's analyze, comrades! Item: the constable's donkey in the communal wheat—neglect. Now let's have some self-criticism," Comrade Secretary repeated, and then fell silent as a rock. He turned from one person to another with a cold and piercing look from his small slanted eyes. It seemed as if he knew everything, as if nothing could be hidden from that devil.

"Let's have some self-criticism." The jaws moved, but the words weren't coming out.

I wanted to tell in detail about everything immediately, but when one met that look, that horrible look, my comrades, one couldn't think of anything intelligent. Everything became jumbled and incomprehensible. Let's see...how did it happen?

...It was during the holiday. It was my duty to see who would come to church, to check how loyal we were to the party line. I observed everyone present and cursed them to myself furiously. Everyone hid his eyes from me; of course, the traitors didn't have a clear conscience. It looked as if God himself were in a tight spot.

"If he wants to, let us discuss religion. Yes, let him do that if he dares," I thought, turning my head proudly in every direction. But she, Itrina, the devil take her, as if she didn't want to know about all this—I looked toward her once, and she toward me three times. I frowned, and she smiled so gently and so warmly and looked at me straight in the eye. Catastrophe! Moreover, she threatened me with her finger and slowly approached me. "And real catastrophe," I thought, retreating to a dark corner of the church. I forgot about the directives and prayed in the quietest voice to the saints to save me from that damned hussy. But she kept smiling so warmly and kindly with her sparkling eyes.

"No, Itrina, no, constable's daughter," I whispered. "Our paths lead in different directions. They will never meet. Yours is finished, you scum, you murderer," I thought; and yet it was so pleasing to look into those radiant, green eyes. My hands clenched, now one, now the other, I saw that they wanted to touch her thick, bright hair, which had the scent of sunflower seeds. I even thought of chewing on her hair. Ah, is it really possible? What should one do?

"And so, dear Argil," her voice interrupted me, "it means, you have begun to believe in God?"

"You know, Comrade," I said and cleared my throat to correct myself, so that I could prove that it was a mistake, that she was not our comrade at all, and that she did not deserve all that. I conceitedly began to strain word after word: "We, Itrina Isailovska, have nothing to talk about. And the fact that I am in the church is no concern of yours. A man can always change his mind in life."

"Ah, yes," she said. "A man sometimes changes his mind. Sometimes a man really does change his mind in life," she said and tried to hide the smile with her hand, a smile coming from the heart.

She was a fox, a real sly fox. But I wasn't born yesterday, either. Comrade Secretary had filled my head with advice for just such an occasion. I knew by heart what to say to her, everything, word for word: "God is a counterrevolutionary and a robber of the people. God is a kulak and a brigand. Down with private property, down with God!" Ah! I knew all that so nicely, although I must confess, while I spoke these words, my heart was tightening up a bit.

"But why, dear Argil, don't you pray like other people?" said Itrina and winked at me, first with one, then the other eye.

"I do as I feel," I muttered, confused and surprised. It was evident that I wasn't prepared for such a question.

"I know what you're like," said Itrina, and, saying this, approached silently like a cat. "I know what you are looking for here."

Itrina was a strange girl and had such warm breath and fiery breasts. God, forgive me!

"I know, my angel," whispered Itrina in a burning voice. "I know all that."

"Ah, Itrina Isailovska," I mumbled, drawing into myself and calling out with a most pleading voice for all the saints to save me from that damned hussy.

"Most Precious God, Saint Petka, Dear Mother, Jesus Christ, Saint Peter, and you, good Saint Clement, save me from the constable's daughter. Amen." But, as if the saints had decided on revenge, not a single one blinked an eye. With no place to turn, a man had to fall on her firm breasts.

That's how it began, my good comrades, and immediately afterwards, I wished to be dead; I betrayed my comrades, I became a cur. A damned soul and a traitor to the Party! But how to say all this, how to keep one's head high, how to look Comrade Secretary in the eye.

"Let's have self-criticism." Only that voice alone, heavy as lead, fell from all sides. That voice struck about the forehead, the head. It hit everywhere and tore everything up by the roots.

That one day—I'll be a monkey's uncle, if I didn't criticize myself thoroughly that day. Oh, that was some self-criticism. Our good female comrades began to cry sincerely, and the men encouraged me with fiery words, and everyone congratulated and embraced me.

"The victory is ours, the victory is ours!" the comrades shouted. Trajče Petlevski opened his mouth for the first time that day and, all excited, said: "Comrades, I, Trajče Petlevski, from the bottom of my heart, propose that Comrade Argil be presented a medal."

"A medal, comrades!" a youth sobbed at the top of his voice. Oh, that was real happiness, that was life, those were real comrades.

"Are you satisfied now?" Itrina met me one day and asked. "Are you satisfied now, dear Comrade Argil?"

"I am, I am," I said with my head held high and, without stopping, walked by, stamping my heels on the ground, my medal jingling convincingly on my chest.

"Wait!" Itrina said in a hoarse voice. "Did you confess everything?" She bit her lip. "Did you confess everything, dear Argil?"

"Yes, Itrina Isailovska," I replied, changing my voice. "I told them everything and now, I confess, I feel much better. Now I feel like a man. My soul sings!..."

"Feel much better." Itrina said, and drops of blood appeared on her lips. "Better, huh? Shame on you!" she said and began scratching her face. "Shame on you, you damned devil!" She wanted to tear at her breasts. "What a fool I was. My God!" she said and sobbed out loud. "How could I let you lay a finger on me?...I'll kill myself, so help me God!"

And so Itrina spoke, and, as if out of her mind, ran down through the vineyards. She broke the young vines in gloom and beat her head on the ground. Then she got up laughing hysterically: "Here, take it!" She lifted her dress, showing her beautiful, strong legs. "Here it is!" she said and pinched her thighs. "Now, I'll go off to the soldiers and lie with them on their greatcoats. I'll lie with them. So help me, I will!"

As Itrina said this, she constantly moaned, then slowly and heavily walked toward the valley. She walked bent to the ground, as if wounded somewhere in the side. She looked as if she would collapse any moment. But she walked away and never again returned to our valley.

This happened in the twilight, and already people were calling to each other to go to the evening meeting. I walked stealthily, taking the most distant path so that I wouldn't meet the comrades. Perhaps I was afraid they would hear me crying. Suddenly Comrade Secretary appeared, spreading his dark, thin lips.

"What's all the noise about?"

"I...I...Comrade Secretary," I muttered, "I'm composing a song, a song about self-criticism. It comes from strong emotions," I said and quickly wiped away the tears.

"Ah, yes," replied the secretary, sincerely. "That's a good thing. A song about self-criticism," he repeated and scratched his head. "Yes, that would really be wonderful...a song about self-criticism."

Then he embraced me firmly, comradely, and, with heads held high, we set out for the evening meeting. The entire way, we sang some song about victory.

Translated by Donald Davenport

SLOBODAN SV. MILETIĆ

(b. 1938)

Miletić was born in Belgrade. He has studied comparative literature and German in Yugoslavia, France, and Germany. At present, he teaches comparative literature at the University of Novi Sad. Miletić has written poetry, prose, and criticism. His first book, *Heaven Without a Title,* was published in 1971. He also writes for various Yugoslav literary magazines and newspapers.

Miletić, a great-great grandson of Svetozar Miletić, a leader of the Serbian national movement in the Austro-Hungarian empire in the second half of the 19th century, writes most unusual prose and poetry. In terms of genre, traditional classification cannot be applied; the author himself refers to his works as "lyric scores." In fact, his writings are an experiment in form, a game of words with an uncommon linguistic originality.

Miletić's ability to master the finest components of Serbo-Croatian, make his satirical achievements covert, but powerful. His poem, "A Big Et Cetera," shows this use and misuse of words according to need.

A Big Et Cetera

Can you imagine what the advantage of Et Cetera is
in comparison to other words
comparing it with "However" and "Between"
and although this Et Cetera
can also mean nothing
or "Between" or "Also" or "Contrary to"
but this is not important
as it is in a meditative poem
of e.e. cummings
can you imagine how Et Cetera
can be a perfect substitute for long titles
and military decorations
how skillfully it can fulfill
empty plains of the spirit
loudly speaking of forgetfulness
between periods and between lines
how it acquires an exceptionally foggy
feature of the undefined
on the paintings of art
but that already belongs to the jurisdiction
of taste
one is to become ill
of such poetic scheme:

a lot of noise about nothing
pouring over from hollow
into empty
a full tabula rasa
will stay for nothing
unsettled settlements
a little bit of extinguished fire
the unsaddled mule
without saddle or master
a handful of pale ashes
too heavy a helmet beardless beard without its master
a breath of a statue
a smell of cut down pine trees
a heaven without paradise
a picture by the blind man
a laughter of the bitten one
a building of the lazy one
a life without sweetness
a heart as a measure
a stomach destroyed
changes summer for autumn
I a shadow
shut up sentimentalists
Et Cetera
and when we forget
we frame it into a portrait
of our annoyed aunt
with a mustache
and how talkative she is
Et Cetera
even more convincing of her
"God forbid" in anger
or at the highest place
of the piano keyboard
our dear lucid
Et Cetera grandma literature
please forgive the words

which are far away from essence and order
I beg you obediently
Et Cetera
forgive us
Yours truly
Slobodan Miletić

Translated by Branko Mikasinovich

MATIJA BEĆKOVIĆ

(b. 1939)

Bećković was born in Senta, Serbia. and studied literature at the University of Belgrade. He is considered the most talented Serbian poet of his generation. Among his several volumes of poetry, are: *A Bullet Wanderer* (1963), *And so Talked Matija* (1965), and *Dr. Janez Paćuka about Time Inbetween* (1969).

The most impressive element of Bećković's writing is his language; it is highly versatile and unusual, quite unheard of in Yugoslav writings for some time. Pure, crisp, inventive, it represents a veritable goldmine for linguists, anthropologists, and other scholars. Bećković's high regard for language is vividly expressed in his observation: "Where talk is loud and speech a festive art, where one talks the other listens, where a man looks the other in the eyes when he speaks, where those who have left behind 'a beautiful word' live on—there one finds the smithy of the language, the source of wisdom, clarity, refinement, and health."

In satire, Bećković has no rival. Though his poems, which are unusually long, focus on his native Montenegro, his satire extends beyond regional influence and becomes Yugoslav, universal. An ambiguous and elusive irony permeates his works. His language is rugged but polished, of rich, heavy texture with a strong popular flavor and a wealth of evocative appeal.

On Yugoslavs

YUGOSLAVS EARN MORE than they produce and spend more than they earn. How?

It's easy. With a magic wand they simply pull out of a hat whatever the modest circumstances of the present epoch cannot offer them.

The bulk of their money they spend on cigarettes, the rest on newspapers. From the remainder they buy:

Pianos, aquariums, fountains, villas, cars, necklaces, paintings, monkeys, horses, vineyards, fur coats, farmhouses, and views of the sea, antique furniture, antique violins, antique clocks, old paintings, old coins, old maps, old weapons, old skeletons, rare stamps, rare firms, rare samples, rare books. They buy friends, mistresses, witnesses, colleagues, war comrades, and life stories; they travel to the most beautiful and the most distant parts of the world; and when they die they are buried under second-hand tombs hewn from the most expensive stone.

Whatever's left over, after these items are paid for, is put into savings accounts.

Staggering!

The Yugoslavs have obviously disengaged themselves from their state, from its problems and hardships, and ceased to be victims of its subjective and objective weaknesses.

The state is constantly experiencing some sort of scarcity: dinars, dollars, credits, prospects, solutions. On the other hand, Yugoslavs have these things, and more—in their savings accounts.

Thus, not by virtue of any scientific or political prognosis, but, rather, through the survival instinct of a vital mentality, the state will wither away, and the people will survive, healthy and alive, beautiful and gay.

Good for them!

Besides: wasn't that the goal of all our efforts and struggles?

We have been witnesses to a variety of crises: in the theater, in exports, in football, in social security, in the coal industry, in education, in the family. Never have there been so many crises!

But these are the abstract crises of newspaper columns, conferences, doctoral dissertations, and scientific gatherings. In practice—for Yugoslavs—there are no crises!

Yugoslavs are finally free. They've been released from their traditional complex, taken a deep breath, and now they're simply grabbing like mad.

Thus, on this volcanic ground of eternal rebellions and illegal activity, a new illegal movement is in full swing—for happiness, for a home with a garden full of flowers, for a bathroom full of tiles, for pep pills and deodorants. The less there is, the more there is; the less they give, the more they take.

Science is lagging, the economy is lagging, statistics are lagging. But no one can keep up with the growth and prosperity of the Yugoslavs.

Children can't wait to be born; that's how far we've come! There are now several hundred candidates for the twenty-millionth Yugoslav. Nothing is more beautiful or promising than to be a Yugoslav.

You've read about it in the newspapers: the number of people claiming to be Yugoslavs is rapidly mushrooming. We hear from them in Austria, Italy, from all over the globe.

The time has passed when the enemy can deride Yugoslavia because of its personal income being relatively low. We beg your pardon, but in Yugoslavia nobody lives on personal income. The propaganda weapon is obsolete.

Yugoslavs work for a salary, and they live on . . . what do you live on, dear reader?

Per diems, separate living allowances, bribes, tips, grants, vegetable gardens, poultry—half for you, half for me? You rent out a few rooms, take a trip to Trieste, and another to Sofia? Councils, commissions, analysis, interpreting, extra tuition, extras on extras? You copy, you edit, you recommend? You do favors, and allow a few to be done for you in return, eh? . . . Admit . . . you have an aunt in America, an uncle in Australia, a sister-in-law in Sweden? You economize on food? You turn the old inside out to look like new? Oh! You sell houses for demolition or is it grave sites or driver's licenses, perhaps? You sold your house and got a rent-controlled apartment from your firm? In wholesale shops you steal retail? Or vice versa? You keep cigarettes under the counter until the prices go up? You sell out the property of a former co-operative farm?

You're doing something, no doubt about it. How else would you live, you and your canary and the piano tuner and the housekeeper and the masseur and the dog, and all those others you lug on your back?

Translated by Drenka Willen

On Success and Failure

THE SECRET OF SUCCESS is best known to those who haven't succeeded. They know all the roads to success. They simply haven't made up their minds which one to take.

They think success is largely a question of manipulation and deception. Through women or by demagogy. Or perhaps by attacking the government at just the right moment.

But when the unsuccessful finally decide to move, they are quickly rounded up and compromised. This makes the injustice all the greater. Their honesty always betrays them. Those who try the hardest never succeed. Those who don't deserve anything get to the top. None of them ever succeeds in proving he got there honestly. Mankind is thus divided into two classes: those who have made it and those who haven't. The former are frauds; the latter, victims of honesty and misunderstanding.

This is where the struggle with injustice takes root.

Is it true every beautiful woman is a whore?

Every successful writer a plagiarist?

Every free-thinking man a paid provocateur?

Every biography only a part of the real story?

Every achievement a put-up job?

Every situation staged?

Beautiful women deserve no credit for their beauty. It comes naturally.

A happy man can't come up with a single genuine explanation for his happiness.

They've done nothing for their success. Whatever they've accomplished could have been accomplished just as well by anyone else, if only they had been talented or beautiful or et cetera.

Success is a matter of chance. A rabbit is fast, but for him to take credit for his speed would be preposterous.

Success is an affront—one man insulting all others.

The successful should be ashamed. Instead, they are proud. And they go around making statements such as:

It's easy to be poor.

To be dumb and silent.

Ugly and innocent.

To be old and withdrawn.

Untalented and modest.

It's easy to be what one is.

To be a miser and on a diet.

A horse and a vegetarian.

A suicide and courageous.

Jobless and hungry.

So they talk, making free use of their talent, intelligence, and courage. They stick together. They have no heart. They take everything that's coming to them.

This tyranny can be countered only by another tyranny. All beauties will be declared whores, talented writers will be pronounced hacks, and free-thinking citizens spies. The countertyranny will lie, set traps, improvise, invent, add little details, embellish....

And more.

Translated by Drenka Willen

On Nations

Are at least two nations essential to the existence of one?

Can one viable nation be made out of several dubious ones?

Can two nations give birth to a third?

Is there a small nation without a heroic past?

Is there enough freedom for all nations?

Is there enough time for each nation to win one great victory?

Can we agree on the world's worst nation?

Are two nations required to have brotherhood and unity at one and the same time?

Can every man be the son of his people?

Is our nation better known abroad than it is at home?

What does a nation think with?

Are there two identical nations?

Is there a nation that no one ever heard of?

Is a nation that continuously changes regimes fickle?

Is there an anti-nation nation?

Why does a nation that never borrowed in the first place have to pay back debts?

Are there nations and nations?

Are there retired nations?

Can a nation be invented?

Does a nation last longer if kept in a cool, dry place?

Can one resign from a nation?

Can one die a natural death for one's nation?

Is a mob a nation?

(Why do small nations always fight for equality?)

To whom does a nation pay dues?

Are there enough small nations around to secure world peace?

Without conquest, would so many nations have a glorious history?

Did monarchies have people?

How do you remain loyal to a nation that has abandoned you?

Is one river enough for two nations?

Is the glory of one nation the tragedy of another?

Are there nations that misrepresent themselves?

Can a nation be greater than the number of inhabitants?

Can a cemetery be a frontier between two nations?

Can a nation start a private state?

Where were so many nations during the war?

Has there ever been a plebiscite without a nation?

What portion of a nation is not representative of a nation?

Is there a nation that isn't always in the right?

Translated by Drenka Willen

On Issuing Statements

IT'S BETTER TO WORK badly and express oneself properly than the reverse.

You may discover a cure for cancer, but if you fail to proclaim it as yet another blow to the power of darkness, to ignorance, to reactionary forces in general, you might just as well not have discovered it at all.

Don't discover anything, but do speak passionately about the need for a struggle against everything—including cancer—about the need to come to grips with evil. Do that and you'll find you've suddenly been promoted to the front ranks of the fighters for progress.

Work is something you have to do constantly; it's hard. Verbal statements, on the other hand, can be made sporadically and are a lot easier. One works out of sight, whereas verbal statements are always made before cameras and microphones. Statements make a more lasting impression than deeds. Statements make the front pages. Real achievements wind up buried in the back, if there's any space left.

We have a poetess of tender heart and small talents who hasn't missed a single important date to remind us that our homeland spreads from Maribor to Djevdjelija, and that we should never forget the unforgettable.

We have a commentator who for years has signed his name to official statements, reports, bulletins, and other people's words. For this devotion to other people's thoughts he is handsomely rewarded and highly respected. There's no danger of his using his head. That's not part of his job.

His opinion never deviates from official statements. His mistakes are never his own, because, after all, his thoughts aren't, either.

One's own opinion is always an adventure, a risk, an unremunerative business.

Supporting other people's opinions is the most lucrative kind of professionalism.

Of course you love your country, your mother, and freedom. But why haven't you said so publicly? You think it's taken for granted, that it's beneath you to peddle your emotions, that it's shameful to get an apartment in exchange for such a public statement.

However, nobody believes you. Others make statements you don't. You keep quiet. Taste? Dignity? Intelligence? Those are your reasons for holding your tongue? Impossible?

Make a statement! It's simple.

As for explaining why you shy away from such an easy occupation, that's hard. Your stubbornness puts you on the defensive.

How will you ever know what you think if you don't make a statement?

You cure people, but don't explain how. You write books, but don't tell us what they're about. You engage in scholarship, but where's the political orientation? You contribute to the glory of this country, but where are you at all the patriotic clambakes anyway?

We've equated statements with opinions. Those who make the right kind of statements think right. There's no other logic.

For our work we receive salaries, but for our statements we can get social recognition. Our work gets scribbled down in our notebooks; our statements published in biographies.

A personal opinion proves absolutely nothing. Make a statement that other people's thoughts are yours, too—everything will be clear. How and what one thinks doesn't matter. What counts is what one says.

One can only think in one way: following one's moral principle. But public statements, public pronouncements, they admit a multitude of views and a flock of moral principles. It all depends. This is why statements are fundamentally infallible.

The more primitive your statement, the more sincere and convincing you sound.

It's taken for granted that people say what they think. Thus, speaking has the edge on thinking. Thinking without speaking has become suspect.

Consequently, one man who verbalizes is always in charge of three who keep quiet.

Those who make statements are equated with progress. Each word and gesture is considered a contribution to the struggle. These sentimentalities become the pearls of the epoch.

Well, here's the recipe:

If you want some peace in this life and a big reputation fast, climb on some podium, hug the microphone like a long lost brother, and proclaim some beautiful and inspiring thought.

Do this and, though you may do little for your people, you could hardly do more for yourself.

Translated by Drenka Willen

On Backwardness

IN THIS DAY AND AGE backwardness has become fashionable. To be backward is to be stylish. The civilized look upon the backward with envy. They are the bulwarks of progress. They are synonymous with health. They are the "avant-garde."

The backward cannot regress. They can only go forward. The backward can take only large strides.

Only the backward have a future.

Only the poor have any hope of being rich. The rich are already rich.

And just as the shabby have more beautiful dreams than the chic, only the enslaved can still dream of freedom.

Thus the superiority of the backward rests on firm foundations. Their future is altogether certain. For they will fashion their future on the past of the civilized, without repeating the obvious errors and blunders.

Hungry and barefoot, full of dreams and energy, the backward will now experience the nostalgic moments of our past. Our most beautiful memories are about to become their reality.

They need no science fiction in their leisure hours. They dream of forks, wheels, irons, their first newspaper, the discovery of film.

They are hungry for things with which we are satiated.

What wonderful excitement, what glorious hunger and curiosity!

Fortunate are the backward; unfortunate those who are not.

Fortunate are those who still seek justice, freedom, and equality. They still have a chance of being courageous, honorable, and celebrated. They are about to have their own poets!

With our experience behind them, they will stage more brilliant revolutions, fight more spectacular wars.

Their Napoleon will be taller. Their Alexander the Great will live longer. Their Brutus will not kill Caesar.

Unfortunate are those who have reached their goal, for they are without a goal.

The free will rot in the immutability of freedom. Satiated with happiness, they will turn to unhappiness.

While the primitive idealize the good, the emancipated wearily search for a new face of evil.

The civilized fill their cemeteries by suicide, the backward by malnutrition.

The rich tell the poor that happiness is not in being rich, but the poor won't listen. Those who have clothes remove them. Those who have no clothes put them on.

Every crumb is a holiday, a step into the future.

The civilized look at the backward on small and large screens and are puzzled by the coldbloodedness that seems to lead nowhere. They would gladly leave their seats and join the game. But it's too late. Everyone can do his bit only once. Nothing can be improved retroactively. One can only go forward, and the backward are doing it.

Let's be good to the backward. Perhaps they will give us a slice of their hunger and a sip of their thirst.

Translated by Drenka Willen

TOMAŽ ŠALAMUN
(b. 1941)

Šalamun was born in Zagreb. He studied art history at the University of Ljubljana and continues to work in Ljubljana as a pro-professional writer. He began publishing poetry in *Perspective* in 1963. His two books of poetry are: *Poker* (1966) and *Cloak's Purpose* (1968). He has also emerged as one of the most distinguished Slovenian satirists; his writings are characterized by biting humor, blissful irreverence, playfulness, and manipulation of verse forms to suit his poetic needs.

Who Is Who

Tomaž Šalamun you are a genius

you are wonderful you are a joy to behold

you are great you are a giant

you are strong and powerful you are phenomenal

you are the greatest of all time

you are the king you are possessed of great wealth

you are a genius Tomaž Šalamun

in harmony with all creation we have to admit that

you are a lion the planets pay homage to you

the sun turns her face to you every day

you are just everything you are Mount Ararat

you are perennial you are the morning star

you are without beginning or end

you have no shadow no fear

you are the light you are the fire from heaven

behold the eyes of Tomaž Šalamun

behold the brilliant radiance of the sky

behold his arms behold his loins

behold him striding forth

behold him touching the ground

your skin bears the scent of nard

your hair is like solar dust

the stars are amazed who is amazed at the stars

the sea is blue who is the sky's guardian

you are the boat on high seas

that no wind no storm can destroy

you are the mountain rising from the plain

the lake in the desert

you are the speculum humanae salvation is

you hold back the forces of darkness

beside you every light grows dim

beside you every sun appears dark

every stone every house every crumb every mote of dust

every hair every blood every mountain every snow

every tree every life every valley every chasm

every enmity every lamb every glow every rainbow

Translated by the author and Anselm Hollo

MILOVAN VITEZOVIĆ

(b. 1946)

One of the youngest and most interesting Serbian Satirists, Vitezović is emerging as a scintillating talent with a wide-based appeal. The exposure provided by the publication of his aphorisms in such Belgrade journals as *The Literary Gazette, The Hedgehog,* and *Nin*, has heightened his popularity. This literary form is widely used in Yugoslavia. According to Bulatović-Vib, "[The aphorism] acts as a fairy tale; when it is successful, it becomes a folk saying. It is also a tiny novel of two-to-three sentences."

Aphorisms

Mental work is physically unbearable.

We placed him as a founding stone, and he became a stumbling block.

A satirist is a state toothache; it is cured by being pulled out.

The most dangerous police are those who ransack history.

When he got out of the trench and into the office, he dug himself in at once.

There is no use in turning the page. The book is the same.

It is easy to give a speech; it is hard to keep one's word.

The voice of the people is not being reported to the people.

It is a miserable democracy when people have to choose between two evils.

During the war he was well behaved; in the front lines, he kept saying to everyone, "After you, please."

Translated by Branko Mikasinovich

Index of Authors, Translators, and Titles

Aphorisms, 148
Aphorisms, 173
Aphorisms, 204
BEĆKOVIĆ, MATIJA
  On Backwardness, 198
  On Issuing Statements, 195
  On Nations, 193
  On Success and Failure, 191
  On Yugoslavs, 188
Big Et Cetera, A, 184
BULATOVIĆ-VIB, VLADA
  Illness, The, 150
  Lavatore and Bureau-
    cratsia, 156
  Municipal Whale, The, 154
  Shark and the Bureau-
    crat, The, 152
  Ugly Duckling, The, 158
ČINGO, ŽIVKO
  Medal, The, 176
ĆOPIĆ, BRANKO
  Election of Comrade
    Sokrat, The, 45
ĆOSIĆ, BORA
  King of the Poets, The, 161
ĆOSIĆ, DOBRICA
  Freedom, 69
CRNČEVIĆ, BRANA
  Aphorisms, 173
  Prosperity, 171
  Write as You Are Silent, 169
Ćurčija-Prodanović, Nada
  Illness, The, 150
  Lavatore and Bureau-
    cratsia, 156
  Municipal Whale, The, 154

Shark and the Bureaucrat,
  The, 152
Ugly Duckling, The, 158
Czerwinski, E. J.
  Hats Off!, 100
Davenport, Donald
  Medal, The 176
DESNICA, VLADAN
  Mr. Pink's Soliloquy, 2
Edwards, Lovett F.
  Strange Story of the Great
    Whale, Also Known as
    Big Mac, The, 12
Election of Comrade Sokrat,
  The, 45
Fenced Sea, The, 95
Freedom, 69
Hats Off!, 100
Heppel, Muriel
  Freedom, 69
Hollo, Anselm
  Who Is Who, 201
HORVAT, JOZA
  Mousehole, 50
Illness, The, 150
King of the Poets, The, 161
KOŠ, ERIH
  Strange Story of the Great
    Whale, Also Known as
    Big Mac, 12
Lavatore and Bureau-
  cratsia, 156
Little Finger, A, 92
Medal, The, 176
Mihailovich, Vasa D.
  Aphorisms, 148

Aphorisms, 173
Write as You are Silent, 169
Mijusković, Petar
  Mr. Pink's Soliloquy, 2
Mikasinovich, Branko
  Aphorisms, 203
  Big Et Cetera, A, 184
  Election of Comrade Sokrat,
    The, 45
  Fenced Sea, The, 95
  Little Finger, A, 92
  Monkeys, 91
Prosperity, 171
MILETIĆ, SLOBODAN SV.
  Big Et Cetera, A. 183
Monkeys, 91
Mousehole, 50
Mr. Pink's Soliloquy, 2
Municipal Whale, The, 154
Norminton, Harold
  King of the Poets, The, 161
On Backwardness, 198
On Issuing Statements, 195
On Nations, 193
On Success and Failure, 191
On Yugoslavs, 188
PETAN, ŽARKO
  Aphorisms, 148

POPOVIĆ, ALEKSANDAR
  Hats Off!, 100
POPOVIĆ, VASA
  Fenced Sea, The, 95
Prosperity, 171
RADOVIĆ, DUŠAN
  Little Finger, A, 92
  Monkeys, 91
ŠALAMUN, TOMAŽ
  Who Is Who, 201
Shark and the Bureaucrat,
  The, 152
Strange Story of the Great
  Whale, Also Known as
  Big Mac, The, 12
Ugly Duckling, The, 158
VITEZOVIĆ, MILOVAN
  Aphorisms, 204
Who Is Who, 201
Willen, Drenka
  On Backwardness, 198
  On Issuing Statements, 195
  On Nations, 193
  On Success and Failure, 191
  On Yugoslavs, 188
Williams, Celia
  Mousehole, 50
Write as You Are Silent, 169

ABOUT THE EDITOR

Branko Mikasinovich is one of the foremost scholars of Yugoslav literature and a noted Slavist. He has edited *Introduction to Yugoslav Literature,* the most representative anthology of modern Yugoslav prose and poetry in English, and *Five Modern Yugoslav Plays,* a unique collection of plays written between 1945-1978. He has also published a number of articles and reviews in American and Yugoslav journals and has frequently appeared as a panelist on ABC-TV's *Press International* and NET's (New Orleans) *International Dateline.* He has taught Yugoslav and Russian literature at Tulane University and the University of New Orleans and was president of the Louisiana Association of Professors of Slavic and East European Languages (1971-1973). Currently, he resides in New Orleans.